• • • • • • • • • • • • • • • • •

"*Myth of the Millennial* is an honest and satisfying conversation put to print. It's filled with wisdom borne of firsthand experience and solid research. It carries insights gleaned from the stories of the very Millennials that many who will read the book find so hard to reach. And it's loaded with the down-to-earth wit of authors who take the Gospel seriously and themselves lightly. Ted and Chelsey's words are so effective at cutting through the stereotypes and offering practical application and pastoral encouragement to all generations that one has to think it will become the go-to resource for ministry to Millennials for years to come."

—Rev. Matt Popovits, Pastor, Our Saviour New York,
Rego Park, NY; Author of Tough Call: A Little Book on Making Big Decisions

• •

"*Myth of the Millennial* accomplishes the delicate and difficult task of exploring the Millennial generation without falling into over-generalizations or negative comparisons to previous generations. Using sound and approachable theology, the Doerings draw us beyond an academic analysis and invite us into a reciprocal and Christ-centered relationship with this emerging generation. A must-read!"

—Rev. Chris Paavola, Pastor, All Nations Church, University City, MO

• •

"As a Gen X pastor of a new church, I consider this conversation to be indispensable. Ted and Chelsey write with a brave energy and a witty vitality. They don't back down from what needs to be asked and answered, meanwhile bringing the reader smiles on every page. I'm encouraged by their bright and ambitious perspective, and all the while am fully 'gospeled' by their relentless passion for the mission to their generation. Simply put, this should be required reading for all church leaders in America."

—Rev. Mark Hunsaker, Pastor,
Praise & Worship Lutheran Church, Branson, MO

. . . .

"What an incredible book! Ted and Chelsey Doering understand that if we want to make a difference, we need to do something different. In *Myth of the Millennial*, they encourage the Church to open its eyes to the ways in which we can serve vital roles in Millennials' lives, rather than grow frustrated with them. Through story, relevancy, and the Gospel message, the Doerings teach us something honest and encouraging about how to best connect and care for Millennials in *Myth of the Millennial.*"

—*Tanner Olson, writer, spoken word poet, and creator of writtentospeak.com*

. . . .

"In *Myth of the Millennial*, Ted and Chelsey Doering help mend the generation gap with stories, questions, insight, honesty, and some sass. Most of all, they show in practical ways that there is much hope for the Church when generations love each other, walk together, and focus on Jesus."

—*Michael W. Newman, Author of* Hope When Your Heart Breaks:
Navigating Grief and Loss *and* The Life You Crave: It's All about Grace

. . . .

"Wow! After reading this work by Ted and Chelsey Doering, this Boomer is not only intrigued but eager to see the wonderful ways in which the Lord will work mightily through those who are identified among us as Millennials. Their high desire for relationships and community, along with their sincere and strong willingness to be mentored speaks volumes about their heart for people—that ministry and God's love is not found in programs, nor in targeting people as projects, but in loving them, getting to know them, serving with them, and sharing Jesus with them. This is good! This is very good. This is Jesus-like. I'm thankful for this work by the Doerings and highly recommend it to all!"

—*Rev. Luke R. Schnake, Director of Ministries,*
Christ Lutheran Church, Lincoln, NE

"Ted and Chelsey cut through the media hype to offer a refreshingly simple and effective way to connect Millennials to Jesus. Every Christian wrestles with how best to share the Gospel with the people God has placed in our lives, especially if that person differs from us in some way. Many programs, activities, and experts promise to be the next silver bullet in reaching a Millennial audience. Ted and Chelsey dispel the myth of the Millennial by helping readers see beyond the stereotypes and by bringing them back to the basics of loving people and listening to each person's unique story. May this book both challenge and encourage you in taking the first steps to loving your neighbor and sharing Jesus with them."

—Rev. Mark Pulliam, Associate Pastor,
Mount Calvary Lutheran Church, San Antonio, TX

"If you're not a Millennial, but care about the Millennials and their life with God, this book is for you! As you read this book, you can do this book. The Church, my congregation, and the mission of Christ will be challenged and strengthened by this work. It's engaging, humorous, solidly biblical, sacramental, refreshing, and insightful. I could not put *Myth of the Millennial* down. Millennials, as you engage with the Doerings' book, you will help your generation, honor Christ, bless the Church, and help the rest of us figure out our life together."

—Rev. Allan R. Buss, Senior Pastor,
Immanuel Lutheran Church, Belvidere, IL

"*Myth of the Millennial* challenged me to confront my subconscious stereotypes and consider some specific ways to meaningfully engage Millennials as individuals who are loved by God. The emphasis on relationships over programming provides a necessary corrective to my tendency to focus on what the authors might call a 'silver bullet' program. The presentation style is engaging and inviting, and the illustrations and stories are fresh and enjoyable, while being specific and authentic. The authors' style, along with the practical insights and questions for discussion, makes this a very user-friendly resource."

—Rev. Al Doering, Pastor, Christ the King Lutheran Church, Kingwood, TX;
Proud Father and Father-in-Law of the Authors

. . . .

"Jesus said, 'Therefore GO and MAKE disciples. . . .'" My heart has ached for this next generation of the Church as I have witnessed them leaving the Body of Christ. This book gives a great map for the actions involved in the 'going and making' of Millennial disciples. It has challenged me to be prayerful, intentional, and passionate for the Millennial generation. As God has called us by Jesus' words, let the insights in this book be the invitation and challenge from our Lord to join Him in 'seeking and saving' the lost."

—Mary Doering, Women's Ministry Coordinator & Sunday Morning Adult
Education Co-coordinator, Christ the King Lutheran Church, Kingwood, TX;
and, coincidentally, I love the authors a whole lot!

. . . .

"I'm incredibly thankful this text is not another 'this generation versus this generation.' Rather, with humor and sincerity, Ted and Chelsey move us beyond stereotypes, allowing us to return to the hearts of actual people and their deep need for the Gospel. I highly recommend this book for those who want to do ministry to young and old, Boomer and Xer, and yes . . . to the Millennial."

—Rev. Brian West, Pastor, NextGeneration,
Trinity Lutheran Church, Clinton Township, MI

MYTH

of the

MILLENNIAL

TED & CHELSEY
DOERING

CONNECTING GENERATIONS IN THE CHURCH

For our parents
Paul & Cherri
and
Al & Mary

Thank you for teaching us to tie our shoes,
for extending to us God's love and forgiveness,
and for forming us into productive Millennial adults.

We love you.

Published by Concordia Publishing House
3558 S. Jefferson Ave., St. Louis, MO 63118–3968
1-800-325-3040 • www.cph.org

Cover image © Eugenio Marongiu/ShutterstockPhoto.com.

Library of Congress Cataloging-in-Publication Data
Names: Doering, Ted, author.
Title: Myth of the Millennial : connecting generations in the church / Ted Doering and Chelsey Doering.
Description: St. Louis : Concordia Publishing House, 2017. I Includes bibliographical references and index. Identifiers: LCCN 2017034618 (print) I LCCN 2017037120 (ebook) I ISBN 9780758658272 I ISBN 9780758658265 (alk. paper)
Subjects: LCSH: Church. I Intergenerational relations--Religious aspects--Christianity. I Generation Y--Religious life. I Church work.
Classification: LCC BV640 (ebook) I LCC BV640 .D64 2017 (print) I DDC 253--dc23
LC record available at lccn.loc.gov/2017034618

Manufactured in the United States of America

1 2 3 4 5 6 7 8 9 10   26 25 24 23 22 21 20 19 18 17

Table of Contents

Foreword 9

Introduction 13

Part 1: Breaking Down Stereotypes

    Chapter 1: Generations 21

    Chapter 2: Laziness 39

    Chapter 3: Entitlement.................................. 57

    Chapter 4: Overly Sensitive 77

    Chapter 5: Us vs. Them 93

Part 2: Engaging Millennials

    Chapter 6: Relationships 111

    Chapter 7: Community.................................. 129

    Chapter 8: Mentoring 145

    Chapter 9: Earning Your Voice.................... 163

    Chapter 10: The Lutheran Opportunity 181

    Chapter 11: Practical Advice for Organizations.........................197

Glossary... 215

About the Authors 217

Endnotes 218

FOREWORD

In some ways, I wish I were a Millennial—specifically a Christian Millennial. Not that I'm unhappy with my lot as an early Boomer. We Boomers, born between 1946 and 1964, were raised in a great time for the institutional church. I'm profoundly grateful to God for my parents from the Greatest Generation, those born before 1928. The church where we worshiped was a large but closely knit faith family, including several blood-related families that spanned two and three generations. Our parochial grade school integrated faith into the three Rs—reading, writing, and arithmetic—and our large public high school operated with a Judeo-Christian worldview.

America has changed. Today's culture is contentious, we distrust institutions, government is ineffective, community is formed in different ways, moral issues have become gray, and the Church no longer has a privileged place. No wonder many older Christians long for the good old days!

Ted and Chelsey Doering lead us to hope. Hope looks forward; grief backward. Perhaps you've experienced grief at the loss of a loved one. We also experience grief when something dear is taken from us, like the thriving institutional church many of us knew decades ago. Put that grief about what the church has lost into the context of generations. Perhaps this will help: most of the 2017 graduates of Concordia Seminary are Millennials. They were only eleven years old when the World Trade Center was attacked on 9/11. Each generation sees America and church from its own unique perspective. Unless Jesus returns in judgment soon, today's Christian Millennials will age and grieve what they've lost during their lives. Now, however, they are young and looking to the future. Just like every generation, some Millennials hope in themselves to make things better, but Ted and Chelsey root hope in Jesus Christ, the only Savior of every generation who gives His Spirit through the Gospel to keep the Church faithful and also make it adaptable to the stiff challenges of the twenty-first century.

Millennials bring abilities older Christians generally do not have. Digital natives, Millennials have grown up with the Internet. They were birthed in our new information culture, unlike older people who grew up in a manufacturing society and are sometimes befuddled by new devices and apps. Millennials value loving and supportive families; many of them grew up in broken homes. They yearn for homes older Christians might take for granted. Many Millennials want to reach across ethnic divides; they don't want worship to be the most segregated hour in America. Millennials value personal relationships, but only when someone has truly earned their trust. As a friend taught me, "Don't tell me what a friend I have in Jesus until I see what a friend I have in you." The Millennials I associate with are more discerning about church and churchgoers than many who grew up in "Christian" America, when true faith easily lost its radical nature in a public culture nominally called "Christian." Millennials see hypocrisies those of us in older generations easily overlook. True, Satan can make Millennials blind to their own hypocrisies, but you'll see that Ted and Chelsey keep coming back to the sad fact of sin in each of us and the Good News that every generation has a Savior in Jesus. That's the Word of God working.

There is a future for the institutional church. I believe it is a great future, but in many ways a future different from its twentieth-century expressions. Accustomed to think of church as buildings and staff and budgets and agendas, our church life can be infused as never before with awareness that "we, though many, are one body in Christ, and individually members one of another" (Romans 12:5). That will challenge us to spend more time with one another, time with no program, no agenda—relaxed time when we hear and tell our generational stories. Together, intergenerationally as the Body of Christ, older Christians can disciple and mentor in ways that twentieth-century meetings with programs to fix things cannot accomplish. While it's in vogue to bad-mouth institutions, the fact is we need them, healthy and trustworthy institutions, especially in the Church. And might we older believers provide financial resources so the mission continues long after we've been taken to heaven? I said in some ways I'd like to be a Millennial. Amazing times are ahead for people of faith. In coming years, the Church will be more clearly differentiated from surrounding culture than in our lifetimes. Just as the wind blows where it will, so "the Holy Spirit is given. He works faith, when and where it pleases God, in those who heard the [Gospel]" (Augsburg Confession, Article V). The Spirit of Jesus is leading His Church into and through new and for us unprecedented times. We dare not "grieve as others do who have no hope" (1 Thessalonians 4:13).

—*Dr. Dale A. Meyer, President, Concordia Seminary, St. Louis*

INTRODUCTION

H i
. **We are Ted and Chelsey, and we are Millennials.** Born in '86 and '88, respectively, we are solidly in the Millennial generation. And a lot of people have a lot of things to say about our generation. You may even have some already-formed opinions about our generation, and therefore, about us. You may look upon Millennials as some form of fantastic beast that cannot be understood. Or you may feel as if you know us pretty well. Maybe you are . . . one of us! In writing this book, we want to help you understand our generation better. Because a lot of ink has been spilled concerning our generation, especially when it comes to why Millennials are leaving the church. For all of these reasons, we think it is important to put some of our own ink on paper concerning this generation.

Millennials are constantly in the news. Don't believe us? Simply walk over to your computer, pull up Google, and type in "millennials." In less than half a second, more than 38 million results are found on the topic. Add some meat to your search. Look up "millennials in the workplace," "millennials in the church," "millennials are the worst." You'll continue to discover a plethora of articles, stories, and websites, all about Millennials. Some will be complimentary, praising Millennials as an altruistic group looking for ways to better the world. Others will tell you that when the world is destroyed, it will be because Millennials couldn't look up from their phones.

As you go through those articles, here are some truths you might find:

» Millennials are the largest generation in American history, clocking in at 92 million.[i]

» They are referred to as "digital natives" because they grew up in the midst of the technology boom.

» 35 percent of the Millennial generation has been dubbed "the nones" because they do not identify with any religious affiliation.[ii]

This final statistic is the one to which Christ's Church should be paying the most attention. That number is double the amount of the same category when compared to statistical data for Baby Boomers, and 12 percent higher than that of Generation X. This is alarming not only because Millennials aren't coming to church, but also because more Millennials—more than any other generation thus far—do not see a need for religion at all.

Often the response to the above statistic is that Millennials will come back to the Church when they start having kids. But our generation is waiting longer to have kids and developing a sincere lack of interest in the Church. The problem remains: Millennials aren't coming back like other generations did.

But this is what we trust: Jesus is Lord of the Church. This book is not meant to induce doom and gloom by predicting that the Church as we know it will not survive the Millennial generation. Instead, it's about an opportunity—an opportunity afforded to us as God's people to continue to share the Gospel. As the psalmist says: "One generation shall commend Your works to another, and shall declare Your mighty acts" (Psalm 145:4).

> **More Millennials— more than any other generation thus far—do not see a need for religion at all.**

As the Body of Christ, we have the opportunity to share the Gospel with people who have never heard it or who have walked far away from the Church.

As Millennials ourselves, we'd like to contribute

some firsthand insight to the bigger conversation that revolves around our generation and the Church. We'd like to share information not found in statistics or reports, but rather, found from living on the front lines. We'd like to tell you the stories of Millennials both inside and outside the Church, making them into more than just statistics and stereotypes.

We want to tell you true stories. We want not only to give a voice to people who have been reduced to statistics—a generation talked about ad nauseam as if it were some kind of scientific experiment—but also to dispel the myth of the Millennial. We want to examine the stereotypes given to this generation in various forms of media and found in the preconceived notions that can quickly develop from these stereotypes.

Millennials are the least-churched generation in our nation's history, and our generation is leaving the Church in droves. Because of this, churches have hit the panic button, trying every new program or process to try to connect with a lost generation. But what if connecting with Millennials was much simpler than hiring new staff or conceiving the next and greatest program? What if connecting with Millennials was as simple as buying them doughnuts? giving a high five? listening? What if Christians viewed connecting Millennials to Jesus as a long game instead of the instant gratification of simple church attendance?

Unfortunately, the tendency within churches is to seek to connect with Millennials because they want their churches to grow. This is a double-edged sword. On the one hand, yes, we do want more people in our churches! Chelsey and I are planting a church, and there have been more times than I care to admit when I have met someone and all I could think was, Wow! They should really come to our church! While that's not necessarily a bad sentiment, I ask myself: Would I still love and connect with this person if I could gaze into the future and see that they would never darken our church's door?

In this book, the focus will be on understanding Millennials. Not because they are better than other generations, but because they are underrepresented in the Church and because they, as a generation, are walking away from the hope of Christ in a dark world. Millennials need the wisdom and truth passed down from older generations—we know we would not be where we are today without Baby Boomers and Gen Xers. Members of these older generations have shown us love and compassion and have mentored us and invested in relationships with us. But we also believe that Millennials are of the age where they are able, in turn, to share some of their insight and experience with their elders, especially when it comes to Millennials and the Church.

> Millennials need the wisdom and truth passed down from older generations.

We are proud of many things that have come from our generation, but we also know that we and our peers have, in some respects, earned our reputations as lazy, entitled, overly sensitive, and the list goes on. Among other not-so-flattering names, we're often referred to as **snowflakes** (and if you're curious what that means, check out the handy glossary on p. 215). And while our generation may have earned its reputation, our hope is that the stories we share in this book will help you see beyond the stereotypes and understand how to better connect with a generation who is generally labeled as inaccessible and apathetic.

> But we also believe that Millennials are of the age where they are able, in turn, to share some of their insight and experience with their elders, especially when it comes to Millennials and the Church.

Think of Chelsey and me as embedded reporters, down in the trenches, bringing you the stories from a generation who is leaving the Church but also searching for something more. These are stories of Millennials who have left the Church and of those who love it as well. We want to introduce you to Millennials who both fit and defy the stereotypes, explore the stereotypes that define our generation, and reaffirm the fact that Millennials are actually interested in hearing what you have to say. We'll even give you some tips and tricks to use when approaching the beasts.

The stories we share here are not meant to become the bedrock of your church's new Millennial ministry program. (In fact, as we'll discuss later, Millennials really don't like programs all that much.) Instead, we hope these stories will help you start asking the right questions so you can find unique ways to connect with this unique generation.

Along the way, we will give you insight into Millennials from Millennials. We will also ask some questions to help you think more deeply about how to connect with this generation. We will include activities that invite you to ask a Millennial questions, because the only way to connect with Millennials is to actually connect with Millennials. In our research, we have touched base with a wide variety of our peers to give you a "man on the street" perspective. Additionally, we know that our generation's pesky slang can throw you for a loop, so if you get confused, just be sure to refer to the glossary in the back.

As you read, you will see things from both of our viewpoints. Ted did a lot of the writing. As a pastor, he thinks about how to engage Millennials with the Church on a regular basis. Chelsey did the majority of the polishing and editing. Ted put words on a page; Chelsey helped turn it into a book. Now, because we are telling stories, we will use the first-person voice. To help clarify who's talking when, we have included the author's name at the beginning of each chapter.

Things included in this book will (hopefully) make you laugh, and perhaps some other things will make you upset. We hope you persevere. We want to inform and challenge you. Our goal is to be as fair as possible, challenging both Millennials and older generations to take a look at ourselves to see if we are holding on to stereotypes rather than seeing real people. We want to show you all of the incredible opportunities you have to connect with our generation and to tell them about Jesus. (By the way, the use of "older generations" is not a derogatory one; it is just a simpler way for us to distinguish between generations.)

This book is divided into two parts: Breaking Down Stereotypes and Engaging Millennials. In the first half, Chelsey and I will tackle the broad brushes used to paint the people of our generation. We include examples of Millennials who break the mold. The second half of this book will give you some great ways to tap into some of the positive aspects of Millennial culture. Each chapter will conclude with discussion questions and something for you to do.

MILLENNIALS, A QUICK WORD . . .

All right Millennials, come over here and take a knee. As we progress through this book there will be moments we want to talk directly to you. At times, this will be a high five; at other times, it is going to be a convicting word. Because we need to be reminded that we do not want to stereotype our elders. Our generation lives in stereotypes every day. The sinful human reaction is to respond in kind, to push back and say, "Well, you made me this way!" This process is a both/and, not an either/or. We did not want to write this book as some form of Millennial angst manifesto.

While we want to encourage our elders to connect with us, we also want to encourage you to connect with them. These sidebars, if you will, are that encouragement and, at times, a swift kick in the pants.

Also, a quick warning: some of this content will be convicting—both for older generations and for Millennials. The goal of this book is to break down stereotypes, which might mean getting uncomfortable at points or challenging a worldview or two. But keep going because the overall outcome, connecting generations to Jesus, is well worth it.

Chelsey and I will even let you in on a little secret: You already have everything you need to engage with Millennials. That's right; you don't need to buy a training kit or a video series or anything. You and your church can do this right here and right now.

Ready to get started?

Cool. Let's take the plunge.

PART 1
BREAKING DOWN STEREOTYPES

GENERATIONS

Ted and Chelsey

THE GENERATIONAL PROBLEM

G enerations have always been a "thing" and are not considered modern. In fact, a quick search of the ESV Bible will show you that the word *generations* shows up 119 times throughout Scripture. In its most basic form, the term is a form of time delineation. It helps us to understand different groups of people, family, and culture.

Generational research, however, came into its own after the Second World War. As companies and corporations sought more and better ways to market their products to the right people, advertising firms built more and better ways to categorize consumers. Thus came about the understanding of generations we have today. For the sake of understanding, let's take a quick look at the major players in the current generational game.

The Greatest Generation	The Silent Generation	Baby Boomers	Generation X	Millennials
Born before 1928	Born between 1928 and 1945	Born between 1946 and 1964	Born between 1964 and 1984	Born between 1984 and 2004
The generation who fought the Great Depression and WWII	The least-known generational moniker	Named for the post-WWII "baby boom"	Children of Baby Boomers	Children of Baby Boomers and early Gen X

The Generational Problem is not one of generations, but instead is one of stereotypes. Cultural concepts of generations are built around how to best sell products to a certain group of people in a certain age range. Instead of generations dealing with the passing of wisdom, knowledge, and love from one to the next, all that can be seen are the differences between the older and the younger for the sake of profit. In this vein, let's talk about personas.

Persona [*noun*]: 1. a person; 2. a character in a play, novel, etc.; 3. in psychology, the mask or façade presented to satisfy the demands of the situation or environment and not representing the inner personality of the individual; the public personality.[iii]

CLASSIFYING DATA & CREATING PERSONAS

Personas are a crucial component of successful marketing, particularly for the departments tasked with sales. These personas help to bring richness to cold facts; in other words, they help to put flesh on the statistical skeletons of data. Personas are important because they do not merely divide target audiences into groups; they provide greater depth and context by focusing on one fictional character who embodies the dominant qualities of the larger group. Put simply: marketers create fictional characters based on statistical research and then think of ways to creatively appeal to that character so the audience it represents will buy their product.

Remember the series of Bud Light radio commercials that aired years ago—Real Men of Genius? One that stuck with me (Chelsey), personally, was the "Here's to You, Way Too Proud of Texas Guy," because I'm a seventh-generation Texan and probably pretty obnoxious about it.

It's fine. I've made my peace with it.

I don't drink Bud Light because I prefer good beer, but after hearing and identifying with that commercial, I certainly thought fondly of Budweiser when I found myself in the liquor aisle at the grocery store. This fondness sticks with me today, and if I ever find myself in a situation where my only beer choices are domestic, I'd be more inclined to pick Budweiser over any other.

This is how marketers build recognition and brand loyalty—by appealing to personas. These personas are not inherently bad for creating stereotypical characters out of audiences for marketing purposes; rather, they are strategic and successful. The danger lies in the idea that people—especially people in the Church—would create personas for certain audiences in their minds and then refuse to look beyond them when relating to members of those audiences.

Meet Millennial Molly

Just for fun, let's answer some questions and create a persona. Let's call her Millennial Molly. Here is the first question:

What is Molly's demographic?

According to Nielsen research, Molly belongs to one of the largest and most diverse generations in American history, with 19 percent identifying as Hispanic or Latino, 14 percent as Black, and 5 percent as Asian. About two in every three Millennials were born in the US. Impressively, 38 percent of Millennials report that they are bilingual.

Millennials are getting married at a later age than their parents; in fact, only 21 percent of them have gotten hitched compared to 42 percent of Baby Boomers at that same age. This may be due to the fact that almost one in four Millennials has a bachelor's degree or higher, making them the most educated—and debt-ridden—generation to date. Many researchers agree that Millennials may be delaying marriage in order to have more time to dedicate to the pursuit of postgraduate degrees.[iv]

This brings us to the second question:

Where are Millennials found?

Nielsen research tells us that the top ten markets by concentration of Millennials are primarily found in the western portions of the United States. As someone who identifies with "Way Too Proud of Texas Guy," I am happy to report that my hometown, Austin, TX, is number one on the list. Texas's other large urban areas, Houston and Dallas–Fort Worth, also make the list, along with Salt Lake City, San Diego, Los Angeles, Denver, Washington DC, Las Vegas, and San Francisco.

Interestingly, the top five markets by concentration of Baby Boomers are all in the eastern portion of the country:

1. Portland–Auburn, ME

2. Burlington, VT

3. Albany, NY

4. Hartford and New Haven, CT

5. Pittsburgh, PA

So, to continue Millennial Molly's creation, we'll pretend that she identifies as Latina, is single, lives in Austin with a few roommates, and is finishing her master's degree.

The job search brings us to the third question:

What is her job and level of seniority?

If she's like the majority of Millennials in Austin, Molly is probably look-ing to work for a startup tech company or a new small business. If she's not part of the majority, she might be teaching or looking to use her post-graduate degree as a registered nurse or psychologist. To get by, she is probably supplementing her income with a few part-time jobs, probably working as a barista, a restaurant server, or a nanny. Her level of seniority is most likely minimal, and her income is probably close to the median for the younger group of Millennials: $25k per year.

Next question:

What does a typical day look like in Molly's life?

Honestly, she's probably really tired and stressed. Between her class-es, her job(s), her social life with family and friends, and her worries about the future (due to the level of student debt she's accrued, her uncertainty about the job market in her chosen career field, and a general lack of clarity in life), she doesn't have much time for anything else, including church. In fact, if she does go to church, she's a member of a very small minority of Millennials who do.

What are Molly's pain points, or, alternately, what are the things that make her tick?

She's probably mindful of caring for the planet. She doesn't use plas-tic bags when she gets her groceries (in fact, she might even shop in a package-free grocery store or skip the store altogether and shop at a farmer's market), and she tries to ride her bicycle or carpool when she has somewhere to go. She thinks recycling is the norm rather than the exception. She is concerned with how her food is treated and grown and has probably joined an organic community garden. She is passionate about fighting injustice in her city and around the world, especially when it comes to slavery, human trafficking, and other abuses. It greatly bothers her, as it does many Millennials, when people in authority abuse their power, especially in the workplace and in politics.

Molly also quite often falls victim to what we like to call "Social Media Sickness." This means she is constantly comparing her messy, sometimes-directionless, ordinary, and frustration-filled life to the successes of her friends. She has a hard time not being envious of her friends who just bought their second, bigger house before age 30, took a dream vacation to Europe, or scored what seems like the impossible: a job that pays well and is making a difference in the world. Molly is constantly evaluating herself by comparing her lows against everyone else's social media highs. She fights feelings of inadequacy daily.

Exploring Molly's pain points leads us to the next question:

What are her values and goals?

After looking at what makes her tick, it might be obvious that Molly values health and care for the vulnerable. She values social justice and conservation and probably wants her future career to include these values in some respect. In fact, if Molly can't find a job in her career field in which she feels like she's making a difference in some way, she will probably choose to work two part-time jobs to support herself while she pursues something she is passionate about. For example, Molly might decide to start making creative content such as a series of YouTube videos or a blog, or she might choose to write a book, a screenplay, or even design an app while she works part time at a grocery store or as an **Uber** driver. Or she might even move back in with family in order to save money to start her own business. Ultimately, Molly values the ability to do work she deems worthwhile and having the freedom to set her own schedule, thus creating a healthier work/life balance at the expense of a bigger salary.

Speaking of family, Molly greatly values connection. Like a majority of her generation, she fights feelings of loneliness. Whereas earlier generations sought to create families for themselves among their peers (as evidenced on the TV shows *Cheers* and *Friends*), Millennials routinely seek older mentors. Friends are important, of course, but many Millennials desire to move home and learn from the wisdom of those who have gone before them (as evidenced on the TV show *Modern Family*). Part of that connection is Molly's ability to access information at lightning speed.

Where does Molly go for information?

Number one answer: the Internet. She's probably an expert in spotting fake or satirical news and bad Wikipedia information. She might call herself a **Redditor**. If Molly wants to check out a restaurant, a club, a store, or even a church, she will absolutely look at its website, social media accounts, or Yelp reviews beforehand. If the website isn't designed well, it's hard to find, or it doesn't contain accurate and up-to-date information, Molly will most likely take her business elsewhere.

Molly probably subscribes to a news service like **theSkimm** and most likely only subscribes to a newspaper or a magazine if it's available online. Like people of all ages, she probably does enjoy having physical books and may even own a turntable and a record collection—but these are curios rather than the norm. She downloads and listens to podcasts and audiobooks on her phone. If she has a computer, it's a laptop or tablet—probably not a desktop. Information is easily available to her— it's at the tip of her fingers at all times, even to the detriment of being over-connected and overstimulated.

These final two questions are probably the most pertinent ones to consider when it comes to getting Millennials into church.

What experience is Molly looking for when she "shops" for your products or services?

Well, before anything else, she's probably going to judge your church based on its website. She's going to cringe at bad fonts, bad spelling, bad formatting, and any and all Clip Art or stock photos (more on this in chapter 11). If she decides to visit, she will probably look for how your church is supporting her values: *Did they greet me and make me feel welcome, but not in a scary, overbearing way? Do they use Styrofoam cups at the coffee area? Does this community of faith seek to serve the poor and sick?*

Many people in older generations have been taught that Millennials require a special contemporary service with colored lights and professional bands, among other things, to attract and keep them coming back to and involved with church. While this may be the case for some of our peers, research indicates those are not solid indicators that Millennials will continue to invest themselves in church. The things that keep Millennials coming back, as we'll explore more fully in subsequent chapters, are, among other things, these: a community that feels like family, sermons that engage and challenge, clear proclamations of forgiveness, and a congregation that takes seriously the command of Jesus to serve those in need.

The last question, then, goes hand-in-hand with the one before this:

What are Molly's most common objections to your "product" or "service"?

Molly would not be engaged by boring, surface-level (dare I say "seeker-friendly?") sermons. She would not be inclined to invest if no one invests in her—that is, if others who already attend the church make no effort to connect with her. She's searching for authenticity in relationships; fake cheeriness and exclusivity would be a surefire way to make sure she never darkened your doors again. Finally, Molly would be interested in whether the church serves its community in some way. Or if she did become a member of a church that did not have any volunteer opportunities, she might seek to create and lead some.

So! Millennial Molly is complete. She's bilingual, highly educated, stressed, kind of lonely and confused, and she's broke. She has deeply held opinions about society, the environment, and social justice. You know everything there is to know about her. She's a perfect representation of all Millennials, don't you think?

No. She is not.

This is the problem with personas: they are not for ministry. I walked you through this persona creation and you probably bought it—hook, line, and sinker. Humans like categorization, after all. It's one of the first things we learn to do as young children (*Which one is not like the other?*), and these personas are handy for putting people into tidy little boxes within our particular worldview.

But people don't fit into tidy little boxes. Not every Millennial will resemble Molly. Some will be completely different, actually. I'm sure you're just the same—perhaps you don't resemble your generation's persona either.

People are messy and sinful. This is a truth the Church has known for thousands of years; in fact, it's a truth Jesus knew very well and embraced. Do you think all of His disciples were in any way similar? Absolutely not. His circle was full of people who should have hated one another on principle—tax collectors, prostitutes, religious zealots, the wealthy, everyday folks—and perhaps they did.

But Jesus called them together, one by one, and told them all the same thing: *follow Me.*

This is the problem with personas: they are not for ministry.

Don't get me wrong: personas can be helpful. And yes, sure, they can also be hurtful. But they are not the point.

Jesus is the point. He is the constant factor in the lives of all people. He is the gatherer of His followers and the Shepherd of His people, no matter how apathetic or irritating or messy they may be.

And we, the leaders of His Church, learners of His law, and blessed receivers of His grace, ought to go and do likewise.

"Be imitators of me, as I am of Christ" (1 Corinthians 11:1).

THE GOOD OF STEREOTYPES

Again, personas are largely created for and used by large corporations that can afford teams of marketers. These teams figure out what their target audience wants, create a persona like we just did with Molly, and then invent creative ways to appeal to the group the persona represents. Budweiser did it with "Way Too Proud Texas Guy," and it worked. At least it worked on me.

Another example of corporations using personas to market to their target audience is the fast-food chain Wendy's. In early 2017, the Wendy's **Twitter** account grabbed on to and ran with a style of marketing that greatly resonated with Millennials: they began **roasting** their followers.

In one of these encounters, a person tweeted this at Wendy's:

"@Wendys Roast me"

Wendy's social media wizards simply responded:

"Get one of your 51 followers to roast you."

Over the next several days, most Millennials we knew had seen the engagement and all commented on how great it was that Wendy's had hired someone with social media acumen. Wendy's was marketing to their Millennial audience by connecting with digital natives while using humor. Instead of trying to sell Millennials on how great their burgers are, they engaged with them in a humorous way, creating a story that went viral and was later picked up by **Buzzfeed**.

There can be good in stereotypes, and this book will give you insight into the stereotypes particular to Millennials, especially ones that would be great points of connection between a lost generation and the Church. These include but are not limited to the following: a desire for authenticity, a longing for community, and a love for story.

Other generations have positive stereotypes as well. The upbeat and can-do attitudes of Baby Boomers have created new, better, and more organized ways for people to engage with one another. Members of Generation X have acted as innovators and as great "older siblings," helping to bridge the gaps between generations. Instead of viewing these traits as stereotypes ("stereotypes" generally having negative connotations), perhaps we should start thinking of them as opportunities.

When we believe *only* the stereotypes or the fictional persona of a whole group of uniquely created children of God, we have taken a vast swath of people and made them into action figures. These stereotyped figures are no longer people; rather, they are only what you imagine them to be.

It cannot be denied that stereotypes come from places of truth. But when painted broadly across a group of people, stereotypes deny the reality of how God created humanity. God uniquely creates mankind. The psalmist tells us that God knew us in our mothers' wombs and that we are fearfully and wonderfully made. Uniqueness is built into us so that we can be who we were created to be. Yet a common thread runs throughout humanity: the image of God. The only piece of creation that bears the image of God is humanity. We call this the *Imago Dei*, Latin for "image of God." When looking solely through the lens of stereotyping, we are denying two things: that God created us unique and that others bear the image of God. If this viewpoint becomes a main source of information about a generation, it only builds up divisions and creates an us-versus-them attitude.

In fact, you may have already encountered this yourself. Facebook is full of shared links that lead to sarcastic songs about Millennials, including gloomy predictions for the downfall of the Church and the country due to their laziness and incessant need for participation trophies. And it's easy, isn't it? Buying into a narrative of scapegoating makes people, sinful as we are, feel better about ourselves. When this narrative is given voice, it leads to other generations crying out about the failures of this generation of entitlement. In response, the scapegoats circle the wagon and begin lashing out. How could any of us possibly understand one another?

TELLING STORIES

It is easy to get lost in the generalities and sound bites, so how do we find our way out? We think it's pretty easy: start asking better questions and really listening to the answers.

The best way to do this is to hear the stories of those who are different from you, to understand life from their point of view. As a wise man once said, "If anyone forces you to go one mile, go with him two."[1] With that, let's start with a story.

---

1 That man was Jesus in Matthew 5:41. You can decide not to listen . . . but, y'know . . . Jesus.

Millennial Monday

It originally started as Mallory Monday, named for our friend. She was temporarily living in our spare bedroom as she reacclimated to the United States after returning from her missionary work as a teacher in Niger, Africa. On Monday nights, while Mallory was with us, we would make dinner and invite some friends over to reconnect. When Mallory got a job in Dallas and moved away, we found that we enjoyed these dinners together so much, we decided to keep doing them.

This was a group of friends all about the same age (all Millennials, of course) who got together weekly. The Monday night dinner has varied in number as some people moved away or moved into the area, but our group was generally no fewer than four and no more than twelve. There was no structure or vision other than gathering together to hang out and eat good food. On the Saturday or Sunday before, Chelsey would send a group text to our Monday night dinner thread to suggest sides others could bring to complement whatever delicious main course she was making.

It was no more complicated than that. Around 7 p.m., people would start showing up. We'd eat and hang out for a while, sometimes playing board games or laughing at funny YouTube videos. It has become a time set apart, an unwritten rule in our house and among our friends: Monday nights are taken. The group text thread is long now, peppered with **gifs** and inside jokes.

One week, my (Ted's) dad happened to be in town for a pastoral conference. The conference was at a hotel down in Austin, but Dad stayed with Chelsey and me up on the north side. He and I would drive down to the conference together each day. The first night he was there was a Monday. Although the conference offered options for social hours with colleagues, I told Dad that I couldn't miss Monday night dinner. He said he would enjoy eating with us, so we made plans to add a plate for him.

Around 4:30 that Monday afternoon, he leaned over to me and asked, "Don't we need to get going for your group? We don't want to be late."

His question was innocent enough, but the connotation made me smile. He wasn't just asking about dinner—he was referring to it as a planned programmatic small group with a purpose, probably one with a vision statement too.

I chuckled and replied, "Yeah, we should get going, but it's just friends having dinner. It's not really a group, per se."

As we made our way home, I explained to him how this was simply a time for us to get together to eat and catch up. It was a little community for us. I could tell it was starting to make sense to him, but at the same time, he didn't quite understand how we had something on the books every week that didn't appear to serve a clearer, more intentional purpose.

When we got home for dinner, my dad did one of the things he does best: he asked good questions and listened. Some of our friends were people he had confirmed as a pastor, and some were unknown to him. He was open to opinions different than his and did not feel a need to defend himself.

Later that night, Dad coined the name of our weekly gathering. In the midst of our conversation, after everyone had left, he said offhandedly: "I had a great time at your Millennial Monday tonight." Since then, we have referred to our weekly dinners as Millennial Monday, though Mallory does like to remind us it started with her. In a very real way, Dad influences our weekly dinners. He has mentored several of us over the years, and this is especially apparent when he is in town to visit. Our friends who go to different churches make a point to attend worship at our church to see him and my mom on these days. Millennials seek out mentors, people who have gone ahead of them.

My parents are *thoroughly* Baby Boomers. I once sat down with my dad and attempted to explain social media. Two hours and several diagrams later, we both decided to move on . . . *quickly*. It's not that my dad didn't get it. It was that we were talking past each other. As a digital native, I took certain things for granted—things that were not native to my dad. But my dad—both of my parents, really—have a keen ability to listen patiently and reflectively. Because of this, they are respected and loved by many people in my generation, including, but not limited to, me and my siblings.

MILLENNIALS, LET'S CHAT.

You don't need permission. That's right. You don't need it. Throughout life, and as we walk through the idea of fighting stereotypes and connecting generations in the pages of this book, you don't need permission to do what needs to be done. Get involved in your church, your neighborhood, your apartment complex. Invite your neighbors or friends over for dinner. Make it a standing invitation. One of the coolest experiences from life at the seminary was dinner with the neighbors in our apartment. Dawn and Eric were a married Gen X couple, EJ was the nurse who lived above us. Some of the best memories from that apartment building were sitting around laughing with these people with whom we lived in proximity. Sometimes there is a disconnected belief that we have to ask permission, to find the "right" way to build community. What we, Chelsey and Ted, have found is the best way to start community is just to start it. We Millennials in the Church can at times revert back and think that someone has to tell us what we are doing is approved or that we are okay to start something. As a pastor, I would have two criteria for anything you want to do: Are you going to love God with everything you have? Are you going to love your neighbors? Then do it. It's time for us to get cranking and throw some parties to meet the folks around us.

Getting into the Trenches with Millennials

Millennials are lost. We are encountering the world in new ways. We entered the full-time workforce at one of the worst times in our economy's history. We (generally) come from backgrounds in which we were taught that we could do whatever we dreamed, and that we were the absolute best at whatever we did. We are quickly learning that it is much harder to achieve our dreams than we initially thought—perhaps because many of us did not have to struggle much as children or teenagers.

Millennials are craving to hear with their own ears that we are not the first generation to hit these realities. We want to listen to the war stories of those who came before us; to more fully understand that there is nothing new under the sun. We really don't want sugarcoating—we simply want to know we aren't alone. We yearn for the knowledge and wisdom you have accumulated.

At the same time, we want you to know that we are adults—adults who value the guidance and wisdom of those older and more experienced than us. We are ready to assume positions of leadership and responsibility. We have been told all our lives to wait our turn, but the oldest members of our generation are in their thirties, and the tail end of our generation is approaching the legal drinking age. Over the years, we have been preparing and are excited for a chance to be a part of the conversation. There has been great anticipation to, metaphorically, have a seat at the table.

Ignore the "10 Reasons Millennials Are Leaving Your Church for a Taco Truck" articles you see online, and refocus on the unpopular truth the articles miss: the Millennial generation, like every generation before it, needs Jesus. Everyone needs the Gospel, no matter the age. Millennials are pouring all of their energy and emotion into trying to fill the God-shaped void in their lives. And while you and your church can try to implement every new program and policy under the sun and start up new small groups left and right to try to attract Millennials, none of these efforts get to the root of the issue the way the Good News does.

We want to listen to the war stories of those who came before us; to more fully understand that there is nothing new under the sun.

That's why this book exists. There is no silver bullet for getting Millennials back into the Church or connected to Jesus. There are no "5 Easy Steps." We wrote this book to encourage you and to remind you that our heavenly Father gave you a spirit of power and love, not of timidity. You have all the supplies you need at your disposal. We just want to help you better understand our generation so you can better use the gifts you already have—gifts you've been given that can help you effectively connect with those outside of your generation, younger or older!

There is a gold mine of talent and knowledge in these young people, and many Millennials can and want to contribute to the Body of Christ. So ignore the popular narrative that says this generation doesn't want anything to do with the Church, or you. Debunk the marketing personas. Tear down the caricatures. Jump into the trenches with us Millennials and declare the saving work and grace of Jesus Christ to the lost.

MILLENNIALS, WE JUST TALKED YOU UP . . .

You've got this. If you are reading this book in a small group or with some folks in an older generation, you are about to become the token "Millennial Voice." But we set you up for that. And here is what we would ask:

- When you disagree with us, disagree. Let people see that Millennials are different from one another. Help people see your point of view.
- Share your story. Let folks know what is like to be growing up in this day and in this culture.
- Admit when you fulfill these stereotypes. It's okay, we all want to keep growing.
- Have just as much of a heart for the older generations as we are asking them to have for you.

DISCUSSION QUESTIONS

1. To which generation do you belong? What are some stereotypes of your generation?

2. Do you identify with your generation's stereotypes? Explain.

3. Have you encountered negative media concerning Millennials (TV, websites, social media, etc.)? What has this media told you?

4. If you are reading this book in a group, is there a Millennial in your group? Yes. Great!

   > Ask your Millennial this question: How do you feel about how your generation is portrayed in the greater culture?

   No. Cool; go find one. We'll wait.

   > You found one! A real, live Millennial! We are proud of you.
   > Ask: How do you feel about how your generation is portrayed in the greater culture?

5. Wait! . . . I'm reading this book on my own. I feel left out . . . Don't worry, we are proud of you too! Find a Millennial and ask, How do you feel about how your generation is portrayed in the greater culture?

6. What is the Gospel? What does it mean for you, specifically?

DO IT

Millennials are leaving the Church. There are statistics, pie charts, and graphs that prove this. But we serve the Creator of the cosmos. The first place to start is praying over your concerns and frustrations. Take this issue, of young people leaving the Church, to the Lord. Pray simple things. Pray that He would have compassion, to deploy His Church to those who need His grace, and to open hearts to the Good News of Jesus.

LAZINESS

Ted

f I had to name the number one stereotype of Millennials, it would probably be laziness or apathy.

A prime example would be the child who returns home after college to live in their parents' basement (or spare room—we don't have basements in Texas) while they work a job only to have enough money to go out with their friends or play video games. Or conversely, the perfect example might be your Millennial co-worker who is always on Facebook. Or it could be that table of young people you see in the restaurant not speaking to one another, all of their faces lit by the blue glow of their iPhones, too lazy to interact together in the real world.

It's been repeated over and over by cable news anchors, Facebook posts, and around every water cooler in the country: Millennials are lazy, and they have short attention spans.

The usual conversation, in media, around coffee, or in Bible studies begins like this: "I can't believe those Millennials. They can't get a job.

They can't keep a job. They won't get off their phones." (You get the idea.) The basic gist is that Millennials have become the ruin of America. Or if they haven't ruined it yet, they will.

This stereotype would have you believe that laziness is a recent development, and that might be partly true if you look only at the surface level of these statistics.

> » In 2015,[v] almost 34 percent of Millennials between the ages of 18 and 34 were living at home with their parents.

> » The median marriage age as well as the age of first-time parents has moved to 30.[vi]

> » Home ownership has declined, as well as the number of cars owned.

This must mean that all Millennials aren't working hard enough to get out of the house and chase the American dream, right?
Or . . . does it?

THE STRUGGLE WITH SLOTH

Laziness is not a new problem—just ask the apostle Paul.

Apparently, there was a group of Christians in the Church in Thessalonica who thought that, with the end times quickly approaching, they could just hang around and not get their work done. Paul had some intense words for them:

> Now we command you, brothers, in the name of our Lord Jesus Christ, that you keep away from any brother who is walking in idleness and not in accord with the tradition that you received from us. For you yourselves know how you ought to imitate us, because we were not idle when we were with you, nor did we eat anyone's bread without paying for it, but with toil and labor we worked night and day, that we might not be a burden to any of you. It was not because we

do not have that right, but to give you in ourselves an example to imitate. For even when we were with you, we would give you this command: If anyone is not willing to work, let him not eat. For we hear that some among you walk in idleness, not busy at work, but busybodies. Now such persons we command and encourage in the Lord Jesus Christ to do their work quietly and to earn their own living. As for you, brothers, do not grow weary in doing good. If anyone does not obey what we say in this letter, take note of that person, and have nothing to do with him, that he may be ashamed. Do not regard him as an enemy, but warn him as a brother. (2 Thessalonians 3:6–15)

Laziness has been around since the fall of Adam. As God created man, work was part of that creation. Adam and Eve were created with purpose. In fact, we can infer that work before sin was purely enjoyable because, after sin enters the world, God says, "By the sweat of your face you shall eat bread, till you return to the ground, for out of it you were taken; for you are dust, and to dust you shall return" (Genesis 3:19). It is in our sinful nature to want to shirk work and spend our time lounging on the couch. The curse of sin has meant that work has become more difficult and less fulfilling; that which we accomplish with our hands and minds becomes less meaningful.

In this regard, laziness is not solely a Millennial trait. Every generation has dealt with these issues. From Adam to Abraham, from Boomers to Millennials, we all need to be reminded that part of our created order is to work, to be creators, following the One who created everything out of nothing.

Our sinful nature, though, pulls us toward laziness. Instead of seeking work, we long for the weekend. Mondays have become the most hated day of the week. But look at what happens when we are not busied with work. Paul notes that gossip is quick to follow. This is such a problem for the Church at Thessalonica that Paul tells them to treat harshly those who do not work. He asks the Church to love them as brothers, but remind them of their need to work.

Our sinful desire as humans is simply to have things handed to us. This is why the lottery is so popular. "You're telling me I don't have to do anything, and I could buy a private jet? I'm in!" It is important for us as Christians to remember that the issues we see in the Millennial generation have also affected older generations. Just look to the words of Solomon in Ecclesiastes: "What has been is what will be, and what has been done is what will be done, and there is nothing new under the sun" (Ecclesiastes 1:9). The trap laid for us is to believe that the sins of our youth are no longer sins of the youth. It is easy to forget that the younger generations have always struggled with youthful sins. As people grow older, they gain wisdom and clarity. But they also forget what it was like when they were young. I have already noticed this with Millennials; we have begun to look down on the next generation for being, well, youthful. It is part of our sinful cycle as humanity.

FACTORING IN INSTANT GRATIFICATION

Remember when the Internet was new? Older Millennials have memories that reach back to AOL disks; younger Millennials know only DSL speeds or high-speed Internet. Remember your first cell phone? Some of you wore them like a briefcase over your shoulder. In high school, some Millennials perfected the art of texting under their desks so teachers couldn't see. For us Millennials, instant gratification was grafted into us. As Internet speeds increase, our ability to wait decreases. It's not that that ability to wait isn't there, but it has been buried beneath layers of fast Internet, fast communication, and fast food. We have built a language around emojis and texts while shortening as many words as possible. Some of what may appear to be laziness is actually impatience.

How about YouTube? Wikipedia? Google? Remember when those were started? I often tell fellow pastors of older generations that their greatest fear shouldn't be that their Millennials will ignore them, but that they will be fact-checked. What were arguments like before Google?[2] Millennials start arguments, and you can be assured we finish them as well. This persistence and need to be right is a by-product of growing up in a world of constant access to information, all leading to instant gratification.

Along those same lines, Millennials have lost their ability to be bored. If we desperately need something from the store but don't want to go out, we can have it in our hands in two hours or less with **Amazon Prime Now**. Dinner at our favorite restaurant would be great tonight, but we want to watch the Golden Globes, so we order dinner through **Grubhub**. We constantly need to check in on Twitter, Facebook, Instagram, and Snapchat. Millennials never have a dull moment because of one word: smartphone. We never get bored because we can always check in on something. If worse comes to worse, and we've exhausted all options, we can always check out LinkedIn. Communication with the opposite side of the world is as easy as touching a screen. Access to more media content than has existed before is now available through a five-inch screen anywhere we have signal. We don't get bored because Netflix follows us wherever we go.

Waiting seconds has become a Herculean task. Chelsey and I have debated cutting cable for several months now. It would save us a lot of money, and we have the ability to watch the shows we enjoy via **Hulu**. What is holding us back? The ability to skip commercials. How could we ever wait the ninety seconds between commercials?! But in our day and age, when the amount of content is measured in gigabytes per second, we have been conditioned, like Pavlov's dog, so that ninety seconds feels like an eternity.

An Empathetic Look at the Mid-2000s

To be sure, there are lazy Millennials. There are people who just don't want to get it together. They want everything done for them and handed

---

2   This isn't rhetorical . . . what *were* arguments like before Google?

to them on a silver platter. But the phrase of "Just get a job!" doesn't apply to every Millennial.

Millennials began entering the working world in force in the mid-2000s. They graduated college being told they could achieve whatever they set their minds to, and what happened? We hit the greatest recession since the Great Depression. At the time, Millennials graduated into a world with the largest amounts of school debt this country had seen. They were looking for jobs to get their start, and there were none to be found. Baby Boomers were working longer because they needed the income as life expectancy continued to rise and retirements looked to be longer because of it. Generation Xers weren't advancing in companies as quickly because the Boomers weren't retiring. Millennials came from college in droves, applying for any and every job they could find in their field, only to be told they didn't have enough work experience. The job opportunities were few and far between.

In an attempt to make a dent in paying off college loans, some moved in with their parents, saving money on housing. Many took jobs that underpaid for their education. In the midst of this, some got married and started families, hopeful the job market would soon swing back.

This was the reality Millennials walked into as they graduated high school and college. At a time when Millennials were being called lazy, many couldn't find work. So, some went to grad school. Others who couldn't find a job in their field moved forward with various part-time jobs or another job in a completely different field. A lot of Millennials got creative. Another group moved home and . . . got lazy. But that was not everyone, not the majority, as the media portrays.

Hardworking Millennials

The stories of hardworking Millennials are easy to tell. They are fantastic men and women who are working diligently where they are to move forward and grow. Here are a few stories of Millennials we know:

- Meredith works at our church body's district office, as the office manager. At age 27, she has dealt with cleaning out old closets with years of old district material, painting the entire office, and managing the fallout from a flooding that exposed asbestos that had to be removed. For two years before this, she was a missionary in China. Let us not fail to mention she keeps a pair of coveralls in her car and changes her own oil.

- Ashlee is a local theater teacher. She also acts in the local community theater, which is one of the highest-rated in central Texas. While there, she has been open and honest about her faith and has been a beacon of Jesus to those who are far from Him. She also coaches cheerleading, sings for church, and leads a Bible study for young women from the local university.

- Jeff, age 29, is the head of accounting for a Division I university. He started right out of college working at his alma mater in the print shop, then as a salesman for an alcohol distribution company selling wine and stocking shelves at local grocery stores. When he got his job in accounting, he shot up the ranks because of his work ethic.

- Ben married into our group of friends. He met his wife, our friend Lauren, in New York City at their local church, where they both volunteered. He works in a market research firm based out of Manhattan. Before he and his wife moved to Austin, his company decided to fly him back to NYC to work with the head office when they needed him. While Ben does all of this, Lauren travels around central Texas as an educator with Texas School for the Deaf.

- Kaley is Lauren's sister. You may have seen her on an episode of *Fixer Upper*. She works in Waco as a social worker. In her *massive* amounts of spare time, she is a foster mom. She adopted her first son last year.

- Josh is a pastor in Chattanooga, TN, and planted a church in the inner city. He and his family moved into the neighborhood and they have been doing the slow and laborious work of earning their place among long-time residents. Day in and day out, he deals with issues many of us can't even imagine: their storage shed was burned to the ground; the bus they use for an after school program, which they had painstakingly raised money for, was rammed in an intersection. Josh also counsels many kids through the pain of watching people in their neighborhood die in violent ways.

The lack of jobs encouraged Millennials to adapt. An entrepreneurial spirit blossomed among our peers, and many started their own small businesses. One of my favorites is a brewery that started in our little town north of Austin. Our friends Andrew and Drew grew up together. After college, they went their separate ways. Drew had played golf in college and became a golf pro. Andrew spent some time studying in Germany, following in the footsteps of his grandfather, who had been a brewmaster there. These two men are now the core of the new brewery that Andrew started in our small town.

We met Andrew at our mother church. The time and effort he put into starting the brewery was astounding. Drew came on as the head of sales with the daunting task of getting their beer on tap at local restaurants. In 2015, Rentsch Brewery opened their doors. There have been good times and challenging times. But throughout, they have worked harder than most people I know to see their business get off the ground.

HOW TO CONNECT

Now that we've explored the laziness stereotype, let's dig in with how to connect with Millennials despite, and at times *in spite of*, this stereotype.

First, if you know Millennials who are working hard, encourage them. These are young people who have pushed through tough times to grow and find their place in this crazy world, just like you did. They may work differently than you do, but they are still working hard. Here are some things to expect when you start connecting with Millennials:

- Millennials probably ask lots of questions, especially about the best way to do something. This isn't because we won't work hard, but because we are seeking a template for success.

    Connection Point: *This is a great time for you to share your wisdom and experience from your own work.*

- We may wear headphones to listen to music while we work. This is to help us get in the zone and focus, not to be rude.

    Connection Point: *Ask them what music they listen to when they work and how it helps them focus.*

- We are likely always tempted to be on our phones.

    Connection Point: *If you lead meetings or group projects, request everyone to place their phones in the center of the table. They will be there in case of emergency, but this will encourage people to engage with one another before, during, and after your meeting.*

These are some great ways to gain insight into and connect with a younger generation. Another great way to do this is to ask good questions. This will be emphasized over and again in this book. If you meet Millennials who are working hard at their jobs, it's probably because they love their jobs or they are working toward a dream job. Let them share with you why they love their jobs. Ask them what challenges them and what has been causing growth. Now, here's the key: listen. Listen even when they sound young, when their thoughts and processes show that they are new to what they are doing. Use some grace because they are young and new at what they are doing.

The Law and Gospel Approach

Now, what about connecting with Millennials who do fit into the lazy stereotype? We encourage you to fall back on what you know, in this case, Law and Gospel. The theological outlook of Law and Gospel is simple. Know your distinctions. Law shows us God's created order for our lives and our need for a Savior. The Gospel is Jesus for us, His death to destroy our sins and His resurrection to give us new life. Law and Gospel prove incredibly useful for Millennials as we grow spiritually, teach the faith, and seek to live our lives in accordance with the Word. Yet a healthy Law and Gospel distinction is also an incredible tool for how Christians can learn to interact with the people around us.

Using Law and Gospel in everyday situations is an incredible blessing. Let's say there is a Millennial you know named Kyle who is frustratingly lazy. He's living at home with his parents, works part time only to have enough money to party with his friends, and wears skinny jeans. Kyle's parents are friends of yours, and they trust your judgment and wisdom. They come to you knowing you have a good rapport with Kyle and ask if you would talk with him. You agree and ask Kyle if you can take him to lunch. (As with most people, Millennials love food. In 98 percent of cases, if you buy lunch or coffee for a Millennial, you already have a foot in the door.) As you go to lunch with Kyle, here is where you apply your Law and Gospel for daily living. Ask good questions and listen to Kyle's responses. As he talks, consider whether he appears to be self-aware, admitting that he knows he needs to buckle down and get a job. Look for ways in which you can encourage him. Ask if he knows what his next steps are for pursuing that plan. Or does Kyle feel no need or urgency to get a move on with his life? Is he living in a world where his entitlement has taken over? Graciously call him out. Bring that Law to him, hoping to convict him in ways he needs to grow.

Here is the thing, Law and Gospel as a daily theological lens starts at 30,000 feet but allows you to get to the ground level with people. While you use this lens to figure out how to respond to someone, it shows you how to witness to them as well. The 30,000-foot overview lets you see the need and an appropriate response. The ground level lets you see if people are convicted of their sin and know their need of the balm of Jesus, or whether they appear blind to their sinful ways. Law and Gospel helps. Always, as Peter writes, "in your hearts honor Christ the Lord as holy, always being prepared to make a defense to anyone who asks you for a reason for the hope that is in you; *yet do it with gentleness and respect*" (1 Peter 3:15, emphasis added). The whole point of connecting well is to be able to share that hope that is in you. Jesus gives the Church this model in Matthew 18 where He explains how to seek after an unrepentant brother. Take a minute to read that chapter and see the depth in which this Law/Gospel lens works itself out in the life of the Church.

When you encounter someone who frustrates you or wants to stereotype you, remember, you are called to gentleness and respect. A healthy Law and Gospel distinction is a good step in the right direction. It will bring you to a place of seeing how you can connect with others, and it will lead you to wisdom in how you can encourage or convict.

A BASEBALL METAPHOR

At some point in your lifetime, you learned something. Be it how to throw a baseball, do long division, or at the very least read (one would assume—otherwise you are just staring at this page). Let's take learning how to throw a baseball. The way it often works when a child starts to play baseball or softball is that they begin with T-ball, one of God's most precious gifts to mankind.

Why is T-ball such a gift? Glad you asked. Watching T-ball is one of the greatest amounts of joyous laughter one can find on a sports field today. All the kids are still young enough that most parents aren't worried about whether their children will get scholarships or someday play professionally. It is set aside as a time to learn. Because of this, hilarity ensues. Joey hits the ball and proceeds to take off full tilt . . . toward third base. Kristen fields a ground ball, winds up to throw, releases the ball behind her head, and it soars into left field. Yet despite all the mistakes, no one is mad at these kids; they are just learning.

As children grow, however, we expect more out of them. Kristen grows up to be a great softball catcher. Every year, she builds on what she knows. Joey keeps getting faster and becomes one of the best base stealers in his league. Their skill sets keep growing. These two keep moving on to the next phase, the next level of play. It is a joy to watch them play. Who has helped them with this development? Coaches. Moms and Dads. Older players. They can see potential in these kids, and also see the same struggles they faced at a younger age. But which is more beneficial? For a coach to grumble about how Joey just can't keep his swing level, that kids these days just don't have the discipline needed to play the game? Or for a coach to pull Kristen aside and walk her through a drill that helps her improve her mechanics as she throws to second base?

Laziness and learning are two different things. Differentiating between the two is important when working or interacting with Millennials. I had a discussion on this with my friend Bill, who is a Gen Xer. Bill is a pastor now, but earlier in life he worked for a cell phone company developing technologies that were groundbreaking at their release and have now become commonplace because of their usefulness. When I asked him about Millennials, he shared that, as one of the younger workers in his office, he was asked to help transition Millennials into their jobs at the company. He said one frustration was that Millennials were constantly asking questions and wanting a guide for how to do things. As we discussed this, Bill walked me through what he realized: at first, this frustrated him because there were obvious ways for these Millennials to get their work done. Then he started realizing they weren't always looking for the easy way out but instead knew that others before them had developed systems for doing this job.

Bill recognized it wasn't all laziness; it was a different worldview. He shared that Gen Xers had to fight and figure out how to do everything that needed to be done, but now these Millennials expected to have systems in place. Through his frustration, he began to see that he could help Millennials. There were things they needed to be encouraged to struggle through, but in other places he could help. He had become a coach.

BEING A COACH

There is incredible opportunity for older generations to coach Millennials. While laziness is a stereotype, sometimes when everyone tells you that you are something, you start to believe it yourself. What Millennials need is not more people telling them what they are; they need more coaches. Remember back to your most influential coach, teacher, or mentor. What was it about them that made them so memorable? Was it that they always let you off the hook or that they believed in you enough to call you toward more?

Here is the Millennial secret: a majority of us don't want to be lazy, but we have been told that's what we are. Over and over, the message we receive from media and those older than us is that we are nothing but basement dwellers in our parents' homes. That accusation has somehow wormed its way into our identity. We don't need more people telling us that; we feel it every time we look down at our clocks and see we have spent another night staying up way too late watching Netflix. When that one project we wanted to get done around the house a month ago is still glaring at us in the face. When we are struggling to be the best young parents we can be but can't seem to be getting a grip on anything. You don't have to tell us we are lazy. All too often we buy into the lie ourselves.

Be a coach, a teacher, a mentor. It might change the way you view Millennials. This is a process that will be rough around the edges. In our household, we avoid the word *easy*. We use the word *simple*. Because simple things can be hard, and we don't want to avoid doing hard things. Coaching, teaching, or mentoring a Millennial is simple. Just do it. But it may be one of the hardest things you ever do.

Here's another Millennial secret (if we keep revealing secrets they are going to take our decoder rings): we want to be mentored. Now, do not hear this as permission to say, "Oh! Millennials want to be mentored! I will go share my wisdom and knowledge with every Millennial!" A professor I once knew used this tactic. He would stop students in the hallway or when they were in his office for a meeting and inform them he was taking them to lunch. Then he would spend that entire lunch downloading his wisdom to them between bites. That's not what we are talking about. We are asking for you to be intentional—to find a Millennial you connect with, one with whom you can have conversations, and one who appears to be open to you. Use your discernment in this matter.

> Coaching, teaching, or mentoring a Millennial is simple. Just do it. But it may be one of the hardest things you ever do.

Here is the importance of mentoring or seeking to mentor Millennials: your purpose cannot be simply to get them to church. In a later chapter, we will tell you some stories about how detrimental this kind of mindset can be when trying to start a relationship with a Millennial. When it's all about upping church attendance instead of relationships, Millennials can spot that a mile away. Here is the truth: Millennials have been advertised to and sold at since they came into this world. This reality has given us an incredible ability to sense when someone isn't being authentic and is instead trying to get us to buy something. When you walk into a mentoring relationship as a relationship—not trying to sell yourself, your church, or your way of life—you are building a relationship with someone, not trying to get them to buy a used car.

The "Old Silverbacks"

Chelsey and I have some amazing stories of mentors who have walked alongside us. Honestly, we could probably write an entire book simply about them and their graciousness in loving us well. You will hear about them throughout this book. Here, I want to share with you the story of a team of mentors: Walt, Paul, and Becky. We were fresh out of seminary, called to Texas to plant a church. There was so much excitement. But then the daunting task hit us: we had been called to plant a *church*. But God knew that and had put in place Walt, Paul, and Becky. Walt is the senior pastor of our mother church; Paul and Becky are a husband and wife who had retired from church work and were integral in preparing for a church plant.

Since our boots hit the ground, these three people have never left our side. Walt listened and encouraged us no matter what. He had the ability to bring incredibly wise words of encouragement and comfort while at the same time calling me to the mats when it was necessary. Paul and Becky encourage us nonstop while bringing their passion for the Church with them wherever they go. We can't remember a time when Paul and Becky haven't made us laugh. They call themselves the "Old Silverbacks" of our church plant. The truth is we wouldn't be where we are today without their guiding hand. They invested in us. Not just because we were here to do a job, but because they loved us too.

A HELPFUL CHART

So you are jazzed up about this mentoring idea but don't know how to connect with a Millennial. Great! We have a chart for you!

Boomers and Xers: Mentoring, coaching, and teaching are your best tools for helping fight the laziness stereotype.

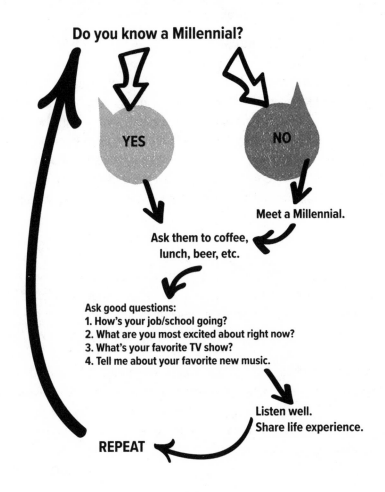

Do you know a Millennial?

YES

NO

Meet a Millennial.

Ask them to coffee, lunch, beer, etc.

Ask good questions:
1. How's your job/school going?
2. What are you most excited about right now?
3. What's your favorite TV show?
4. Tell me about your favorite new music.

Listen well.
Share life experience.

REPEAT

MILLENNIALS, COME OVER HERE AND JOIN US BY OUR SOAPBOX.
This is also our problem. We'll dive into entitlement in a later chapter. That will be a long soapbox; this is a short one. Let's stop thinking that laziness is how we rest. Let's stop being prideful in the latest Netflix show we binged watched or the amount of time we spent beating that last level of whatever game. Let's take ownership in this stereotype and show the world we aren't a bunch of lazy lumps who are only working so we can lounge around when we're not. Chelsey and I are proud to be a part of a generation coming into its own in the workforce, in churches, and as parents. Let's encourage one another to not buy into the lies we're told about ourselves and keep fighting laziness!

FIGHT THE STEREOTYPE, LOVE THE PERSON

Laziness is not going to stop being a problem. It isn't a generation problem; it's a sin problem. Until Jesus returns, there'll always be a want to seek laziness over productivity. But good coaches, mentors, and teachers are gifts from God who help fight the temptation to remain in sloth.

MILLENNIALS . . .
Share your stories of working hard with those in older generations. Let them see and empathize with you. Don't do it in a patronizing or sarcastic way, as is our inclination to do. Let them see the incredible things you and your friends are doing.

Voices will constantly blare the message that Millennials are lazy. Fight that notion. Arm yourself with knowledge by meeting Millennials who are grinding day to day, working hard to continue their growth. When you meet Millennials who fit that stereotype, look to see whether they need conviction or encouragement. Remember the whole reason you are doing this is in the hope that you will get to share the Gospel with them.

Discussion Questions

1. Is there anything that caught you by surprise in this chapter? What was it? Why did it surprise you?

2. Do you know any Millennials who are working hard? Share their stories.

3. Who are some Millennials you can encourage in their work? How can you do that?

4. How can you go about your day using a Law/Gospel lens?

5. Millennials, what frustrates you about the lazy stereotype? Are there any ways you have bought into the lie?

Do It

Boomers and Gen Xers: *Connect with Millennials whose stories you want to hear. Listen and ask good questions about their work and passions.*

Millennials: *Write down a question on which you are seeking wisdom. Find a Boomer or Gen Xer who you think can give you that wisdom and ask them the question.*

ENTITLEMENT

Ted

It is gaining the same notoriety as the famous duos of Abbott and Costello, Ricky and Lucy, and possibly even peanut butter and jelly! *It* being the duo of "Millennial" and "participation trophy." I am getting to the point where I don't even need an egg timer, just another YouTube video of a news segment on Millennials. Your eggs will be done about the time the person begins ranting about participation trophies. This has become a favorite trope of anyone commenting on Millennials, firmly connected to the stereotype of entitlement. Entitlement has become synonymous with Millennials, but there is more depth to this issue.

I decided to ask some friends about their experiences with entitlement. Here are some of their responses:

> **"** *Some Millennials . . . grew up with parents who, with good intentions, gave their kids everything and/or told them they could do/be/have whatever they want, and as a result most of them have a sense of entitlement. What was frustrating for me growing up was seeing that group of Millennials get whatever they wanted handed to them without working for it. What's frustrating and sad now is that those same entitled Millennials are in the real world, . . . struggling, and often times complaining [because] they no longer get things handed to them."*

> **"** *The underlying culture of blanketing ALL Millennials as entitled (or any other 'cultural defect') is hard when people don't take time to get to know YOU; a Millennial. I have experienced people assuming things like this about Millennials while I am in a discussion with them. They don't ask my opinion on the issue."*

> **"** *First off, I find it frustrating that I am in the age range of Millennials. 'Millennial' has been used as a negative term in a lot of things lately. I think partly Millennials are viewed so negatively because of social media and technology. The world is constantly changing and this just happens to be what the world is while we're growing up."*

> **"** *Buy me a beer and I can tell you about all the experiences I've had."*

It's pretty clear that many Millennials deal with being labeled as entitled. It took only an afternoon to get a good number of responses. Millennials feel that entitlement has been placed on our shoulders as a sin specific to our generation.

THE PROBLEM OF ENTITLEMENT

Entitlement is bad. End of section.

Just kidding. You are entitled to a deeper discussion on the topic.[3]

For this discussion, let's define *entitlement* as "the belief that you have the right to a privilege or a thing that you desire." You deserve _____ simply because you exist. This ties back into our discussion on laziness and the apostle Paul's thoughts on working and eating, namely that you should work so you might eat. The entitlement argument against Millennials goes that our generation believes we deserve our hearts' desires simply because we are Millennials. There are plenty of stories of Millennials in the workplace, in organizations, or simply in everyday life feeling entitled to . . . well . . . whatever it may be. Often, the term *snowflake* gets thrown around to label these young people who think they deserve this or that without really working for it. For many people outside our generation looking in, they say we simply don't understand the real world, for you have to earn what you get!

But let's quickly agree on two things:

1. Entitlement is detrimental to our society.

2. Entitlement is detrimental to Millennials.

3. Entitlement is not solely a Millennial problem.

My apologies, I snuck number three in there on you . . . **#sorrynotsorry**.

If we as Christians truly believe that we live in a fallen world, then failure has to be a part of the theological lens through which we view the world. In fact, Christians believe that Jesus came because we failed. But entitlement would ignore that fact. It would say that we cannot fail because we deserve success. But how do we learn if we are not able to fail?

Entitlement robs people of one of the greatest learning experiences in their lives: failure, often one of life's greatest teachers. Failure allows

---

3   See what I did there? You can address any problems you have with this bad joke to me via Twitter; just tag @theo_d.

for the understanding that one cannot do all things alone, that we are in need of community. It teaches that you aren't good at everything, that some things should be left to others. That failure does not end your life—and this is probably its greatest lesson. I could fill a book with the names of inventors, mathematicians, pastors, teachers, carpenters, architects, lawyers, doctors, actors, painters, musicians, and so on, who became who they were because they failed.

A MILLENNIAL ISSUE

Once again, we return to living in an age of instant gratification. From fast Internet to fast food, Millennials have been trained with an almost Pavlovian response to want things quickly. This has translated into our daily lives and places of work. We often wonder, Why should I wait for the dog? the house? the spouse? the car? I deserve them all now. What about that promotion at work?! I deserve to be working in my dream job, not some place where I slug it out to simply make a living. Instant gratification in so many facets of life has led Millennials to believe that things generations before us have worked and waited for are things we deserve now.

Deserving what has not been worked for is a Millennial issue, as it has been an issue with every generation. Whether you encounter this problem in the workplace or on social media (or both), Millennials' sense of entitlement can rob their elders of any feelings of connection or hope for the next generation. But repeat after me: this is not everyone. Don't lose hope by believing that every Millennial you meet is living in self-entitlement. Remember that for those "special" Millennials who are lost in self-entitlement, there is an incredible one-step process for how to deal with them: pray for them.

Growing up in the shadow of participation trophies did not help Millennials with their issue of entitlement either. Let's use participation trophies as an overarching idea. Many Millennials grew up with parents who wanted them to find one thing: their happiness. The driving idea behind the participation movement was that kids would be happy. This isn't completely a bad idea, for it's important to learn that winning isn't everything; remember, failure can be a valuable teacher. But in the participation movement, which spawned the participation trophy phenomena, there is no room for failure. Instead of participation becoming a way for you to learn and grow, it became a way to make you happy. Kids were taught that their happiness was what mattered most, not growth as a person. The experiences of winning and losing, success and failure, were sacrificed to the idol of happiness. This has translated into an issue in workplaces across our country. Millennials struggle with work because they are constantly asking this question: does this make me happy?

Is Entitlement Truly a Millennial Issue?

Earlier in this chapter, you agreed with me that it wasn't. Think about this: for a long time, the greatest desire in our land has been the American Dream—the idea that if you work hard enough you can get your house, your spouse, and your 2.5 kids. The goal of the American Dream wasn't the betterment of society or culture but your pursuit of happiness. Entitlement is not a new concept.

Entitlement has been present since the fall. Adam and Eve were tricked into believing they were entitled to the knowledge of good and evil—and look at how that has worked out for us.

> The experiences of winning and losing, success and failure, were sacrificed to the idol of happiness. This has translated into an issue in workplaces across our country.

In fact, in the Book of Exodus, we read about the Israelites complaining to God because they weren't getting all the things to which they felt entitled. They were rescued from slavery and taken out from oppression. But as soon as the going got rough on the road to freedom, they looked back fondly on their captivity. Why? Because they thought they were entitled to a certain level of comfort, to a certain level of ease. But throughout Scripture, God proves time and again that life is not about our happiness. It's about following Him.

A perfect example of this is John the Baptist. There's a YouTube video of a three-minute segment of a talk given at a conference. In this segment, the speaker tears down the prosperity Gospel through the story of John the Baptist. His message goes something like this: John does what God calls him to do. The Bible tells us John was the greatest born of man (Matthew 11:11). John followed and had his head chopped off because Herod made a promise to a dancing girl. The speaker then ends with, "Follow God, it might end badly!"[vii] John is not entitled; he is faithful.

Yet, entitlement is a sin every generation carries, and it rears its ugly head more often than we prefer. Millennials do not hold the sole torch of entitlement; it is owned by every generation since the fall of Adam and Eve.

While participation trophies certainly have had a negative effect on my generation, they didn't completely ruin us. Here are just a few of the successful people from the Millennial generation who are well-known athletes and entertainers: Michael Phelps, LeBron James, Alex Morgan, JJ Watt, and a majority of the roster of the 2016 Chicago Cubs World Series team. Not into sports? How about Emma Stone, Ryan Gosling, Lin-Manuel Miranda, and Taylor Swift? The Millennial generation is full of people who have succeeded, who have battled their way through adversity, failure, wins, losses, and many obstacles to become great in their fields of athletics, entertainment, and business. This is not a generation totally made of entitled snowflakes.

But it's not all about celebrities either. I have seen Millennials shun entitlement to engage this world for Jesus. My friend Josh, whom I mentioned in the previous chapter, followed God to start a church in Chattanooga's inner city. As a fellow church planter, let me tell you, Josh is following and trusting God. The Body of Christ needs to plant more churches in impoverished areas; the problem is we must continually raise support for these new churches. Josh works, but not because he feels entitled to a paycheck or a platform to become some kind of celebrity pastor. Instead, day in and day out, he walks the long road of obedience to bring the Gospel to the neighborhood where God has called him.

Mark and Laura live in a little house in San Antonio. They are a ministry team at their church. Mark is a pastor, and Laura leads the youth and discipleship programs. They have built an event around helping middle school students and high schoolers go out into the community to serve and share the Gospel.

Tanner is a talented poet and writer. We get together once a week to grow in our faith and check in on each other. When it comes to self-discipline, I know of very few people like Tanner. He has a system for shutting out the distractions and getting down to business. He doesn't believe anyone owes him anything, so he hustles every day. His self-discipline is incredibly simple but effective. He makes a plan for what he wants to accomplish, and then he closes out every extra tab on his computer and sets his phone facedown on the table. When his phone rings, even then he answers it only if it's from someone he is expecting or his wife; he generally won't use his phone or open a new Internet tab until he accomplishes his task.

Jon is the co-planter at our church. He's my right-hand man. When I called him and told him how much I wanted his help in planting our church, he was just as excited as I was. Then I told him over and again that I couldn't pay him full-time. He said that was good. He wanted to work bi-vocationally—he wanted to get to know his community. He now works at Rentsch Brewery. He is trained in church work and is also the director of packaging. All this because Jon didn't feel as if he was entitled to anything.

My sister Anna is one of the smartest people I know. After graduating from college, she wanted to go to medical school to become a physician's assistant. The first time she applied to the top-tier schools, she was accepted by none, rejected by all. Instead of wallowing in self-pity and thinking she had the right to be in med school, she put her nose to the grindstone and worked for a year in the medical field as a unit clerk. She now has a master's degree as a physician's assistant from Yale School of Medicine.

This generation is coming into their own and learning to put the ways of their youth behind them.

THE OTHER SIDE OF ENTITLEMENT

In addition to participation trophies, there is another aspect to this entitlement issue prevalent in the Millennial generation. In fact, it is so closely related—yet at the same time quite opposite—that I like to think of it this way: entitlement is like a quarter you flip. On one side is participation trophies; on the other side is anxiety. More Millennials have been diagnosed with anxiety than any other generation.[viii] Many Millennials Chelsey and I personally know have been on antidepressants since high school. There are several different factors that enter into this generational anxiety, and I'll cover what I believe to be the big three: societal and economic pressures, perfectionist tendencies, and social media.

Societal and Economic Pressures

Millennials are pursuing higher education and advanced degrees at an increasing rate. If a bachelor's degree was the new high school diploma for Gen X, a master's has become the new bachelor's. More and more Millennials are going back to school or simply just staying in school.

The reasons for the pursuit of higher education are varied, but a major part of this movement is that there are fewer jobs available at lower wages than when their parents entered the workforce. As we mentioned before, Boomers are retiring later. Which means that Gen Xers are not getting promotions as quickly. In turn, Millennials have fewer jobs to pursue. Research shows that Millennials who do enter the workforce are making 20 percent less than their Boomer parents (adjusted for inflation).[ix] Careers are harder to come by, and those jobs pay less than expected.

This brings us to going to school. The cost of higher education continues to grow. When Millennials decry the cost of attending university and seek ways to work on student debt, it's not simply because they aren't managing their money well. From 1975 to 2015, the price of attending a public four-year university rose by 149 percent.[x] The possibility of working through college continues to shrink. Minimum wage jobs, those most available to college-age students, can no longer cut it. Because of this, from 2003 to 2016, the amount of student-based debt has skyrocketed nationally from $240 billion to $1.2 trillion.[xi] You read that right. Trillion, with a *T*.

Entering a hard job market with looming debt has taken its toll on this generation. Who wouldn't have anxiety when the first thing you have to do when entering the working world is to pay off the debt you accrued to get there? What about when your starting salary doesn't seem to cover the essentials as prices continue to rise in rent, groceries, and everyday items? All of these factors combine to place stress on any person, and for many Millennials there is an additional stressor: the need to be perfect.

Perfectionist Tendencies

Look at this as the anti-participation trophy. While we have discussed the participation movement, lurking in the corner is its prettier but equally devastating sibling, perfectionism. While, once again, not a new thing, perfectionism was placed on many Millennials by parents who wanted them to be happier. While the participation movement sought to shield Millennials from failure, perfectionism came charging down the hill to the battle cry, "Failure is not an option! Because we want you to be happy! If you fail you won't be happy! DON'T YOU WANT TO BE HAPPY?!"[4] This took root in everything from grades and sports to youth groups and church movements. Working your hardest wasn't good enough; you had to be better. Better grades to make it into a better school. Better athletic achievements to receive a better scholarship, or even more, to make it to

---

4   It was a long battle cry.

the pros. Better in your religious life so you would be a shining example of the Christian faith.

What did Millennials take away from all this? We are never good enough. No matter what we do, we can never attain the love of our parents because they want us to be at the next level. Or worse, God will not love us until we are better. This is legalism cloaked as perfectionism. If only we were a little more missional, liturgical, or pure, then . . . THEN . . . God would love us!

Perfectionism creates a constant state of anxiety. We are never good enough, so we are always worried about being better.

Social Media

Social media is an incredible technology that allows us to connect with people from across the globe. Yet with this interconnectivity comes a hyper form of comparison.

Social media has become a major factor in Millennial anxiety. If you are on social media, when was the last time you posted something bad—something that puts you in a negative light—on Facebook or Twitter or Instagram? Are you more likely to post a picture of the great time you are having on the beach or the dinner you burned, again? Social media is a place to show how great your life is going, not the reality of your life. Millennials connect via social media, and what do they see? How much better everyone else's lives are going. The framed shot that shows the beautiful sunset or the beautiful person or the beautiful . . . you get the picture. All of a sudden, the question is "Why is everyone else's life going so well and mine isn't? Don't these people have any problems?" Jealousy and loneliness quickly combine to create a new form of anxiety. Comparison has always been a form of anxiety, but now it's in-your-face, 24/7, with you everywhere you go in the form of a little blue app with a white *f*.

Anxiety is an issue for all generations. Jesus speaks about it often. But for Millennials, it is quickly becoming a leading, diagnosed issue. I encourage you to look past apparent and perceived entitlement to see if there is a way for you to love a Millennial around you.

A quick recap so far:

» Entitlement is a stereotype. Not every Millennial is struggling with entitlement.

» Entitlement is present in all generations. Adam and Eve felt they were entitled to the knowledge of good and evil.

» Perfectionism is also a problem. Millennials are dealing with a higher level of diagnosed anxiety because they do not believe they are reaching their full potential. Jesus constantly reminds us not to be anxious because He is greater than our fears.

FINDING THE GOOD

Will you find entitled Millennials? Yes. Just as you will find entitled Baby Boomers, Gen Xers, and other generations to come. The Millennials' expressions of their entitlement can be frustrating to the point of wanting to exert some physical energy (read punching bag). A while back, Chelsey and I came across a blog post written by a Millennial that was somewhere along the lines of "Why Millennials Are Leaving Your Church." We are not against someone in our generation taking a look at the issues that the Church faces in connecting with it. Otherwise we wouldn't spend the time and energy writing this book. However, this blog post screamed Millennial entitlement. I believe the author had good intentions and had some fair points, but everything he wrote was about how the Church, that is, the older generations in the Church, could fix things for the Millennials to come back. This blog, as many others, laid out the problems but then wanted their fixes. They wanted a smaller church budget so more could be given to the poor, but they wanted more staff to run Millennial programs. They wanted the church to feel more inviting and welcoming, all while standing to the side and telling others how to do it.

• •

MILLENNIALS, LET'S HAVE A QUICK SIDEBAR . . .

Don't ask other people to fix the problems you see. We are old enough to tackle problems. As one of our pastor friends says, let's move from having good ideas (here's what should be done) to having **GREAT** ideas (what we can do to make something happen). Offer to help. Instead of saying, "Our church doesn't give enough to the poor," find a ministry, organization, or cause worth supporting. Come to the table and say, "I have a group of friends ready to support _____; could we sell some delicious snacks in the lobby for a couple of weeks to support it?" Know about said organization and why they are worth supporting, and share those reasons. It is time for us to stop seeking to have our needs met and time to start giving sacrificially to the Church.

• •

Boomers and Gen Xers, Millennials want to serve. They want to be involved. But if your response to them is to either drown them out because they aren't experienced enough or only tell them why their idea is bad, you will be tearing down the next generation of the Church. Channel their energy. I am not saying that you should simply agree to everything they suggest, but find places for Millennials to lead. Give them opportunities to fail. These chances will battle entitlement. Instead of berating them for failure, walk them through it. Share a time when you failed. Let them know that they are not alone on an island. You have an incredible opportunity to mentor and coach those younger than you. You have failed, and you have succeeded. You can guide and walk along the paths that Millennials are seeking to trod. But they are no longer the kids following behind you; they are the young people you raised them to be! Give them some chances, and help them when they make mistakes. For those who are believers, remind them constantly of the identity they have in Jesus, sealed at the waters of Baptism. The enemy will seek to make them forget that identity. Baptism is God's perfect promise that their identity is always buried in Him. If they aren't believers, encourage them. Keep telling them they're not alone. Help them see their weaknesses and to grow in their strengths. Be always observant to "honor Christ the Lord as holy, always being prepared to make a defense to anyone who asks you for a reason for the hope that is in you; yet do it with gentleness and respect" (1 Peter 3:15).

Again, find the good. There will be plenty of opportunities to witness entitled behavior. Boomers and Gen Xers, help open opportunities for Millennials to lead. Whether it is in your church, your school, or your business, when Millennials lead, you will automatically have a way to connect to the younger generations. Millennials are now getting to the age where they can serve as elders, lead mission trips, work with students, lead projects, and run businesses. There are so many opportunities for them and for you!

MILLENNIALS, HAVE AN ADVENTURE.

Fight it. Allow yourselves to fail. Recognize that you don't deserve the world handed to you on a platter. Besides, what would be the adventure if it were simply given to you? The best stories include conflict and problems that need to be overcome. Let's work to shift our attitudes from seeking our happiness to seeking our best stories. Stories that include hard work and failure. Failure is a great teacher; don't be afraid when it comes because it will help you grow.

THE ALTRUISTIC MILLENNIAL SPIRIT

Millennials share a common streak of wanting to help others. They do this in many forms and fashions. From how they conduct their daily lives to what they buy, there are many different ways in which Millennials seek to give back. Millennials are more willing to spend a higher amount of money on a product if they know that it will benefit others. Why would such an entitled generation value giving back so highly? The simple answer is not all Millennials are entitled.

Connecting with Millennials via social justice, service, and volunteering is an incredible opportunity for the Church. While we are ruled by neither social justice nor a volunteer organization, those things are part of our makeup. Millennials deeply connect with these things God says in His Word: that the true religion He values is one that cares for widows and orphans (James 1:27); that we are to do justice, love mercy, and walk humbly with Him (Micah 6:8); and that the second greatest commandment is to love our neighbors as ourselves (Matthew 22:39). What then are you doing in these areas? Some things may be focused on church-based events such as worship services, Sunday School, VBS, or keeping the grounds around the building. Have you looked around and thought, Do we have any of our young (Millennial age) people serving in these positions? There is such a wide variety of positions! Invite your younger members to serve as greeters, ushers, soundboard operators, and with Communion preparation or assistance. Plug your Millennials in as Sunday School teachers, song leaders at VBS, or put them in charge of a cleanup day around the church. Try using their assistance with new media avenues. For example, use Millennials to help run your website, Facebook page, or maybe even start an Instagram account. Pair them up with someone as an apprentice. Not sure they can handle planning and executing the church Christmas party/picnic/be an elder? Team them with the folks who have been doing it. Put them in a position so that there are those who can teach and guide them. Allow for failure, but not debilitating failure. Instead, instill in them the understanding that sometimes things go wrong, but it's what you do about it next that matters.

What about Millennials outside of your church? They are probably not going to jump at the bit to serve on the altar guild. What is your church doing to serve those outside herself? In fact, let's make this personal: what are you doing to serve people outside the Church? Your answers probably vary greatly. Some of you are serving in everyday capacities: getting to know your neighbors, serving on the local PTA, joining local clubs and organizations. These are all good things. Some of you are working with more complex issues. Maybe you've joined the board of a local nonprofit or enjoy helping with house builds for Habitat for Humanity. Invite Millennials to join you in these things. You know what service opportunities give you? Time to talk. I got to know some amazing people in the times I went on a mission trip or served in my city. Ask good questions, listen to the hearts of the Millennials in your neighborhood, share your experiences, and always be prepared to proclaim the hope you have in Jesus.

This is not a silver bullet. Don't think that any and every Millennial is going to want to serve with you or serve in the way you want them, but simply offer them invitations. Some may decline, but that is okay. In fact, that is how it is supposed to be! As Christians, our job is not to make every connection happen, but instead to keep seeking out opportunities, watching to see relationships form. It may take time, but invest well in new relationships. Get to know Millennials in order to hear their passions so that you can connect them to service in the right areas.

THE FIGHT AGAINST MILLENNIAL ANXIETY

Older generations, we need you. No matter how many times the media says that we are entitled, no matter how many times we act as the worst versions of our stereotypes, we need you. I have seen it over and again on social media over the past several months. I've heard it talking to my friends as they walk through the beginnings of work, family, and life. We feel alone. All we see are people who "get it right." All that is placed in front of us are examples of people whose experiences have allowed them to move past the failures of early life, or the carefully curated galleries displaying only the best of people's lives. Let us see who you are; show us we are not alone on the island. We're begging for people to be real with us because everything else seems fake.

Our friend Keri is doing just that. Keri is a young Millennial mother of three. In her early years of mothering she made a conscious decision: her social media feeds would not show only the best, they would show reality. I love seeing Keri's posts because she is a great mom. Not because she always gets it right, but because she understands that she does not. And in not being perfect, she teaches her kids so many and varied things. They just got two rabbits in the past month. Listen: if you want to find joy, just watch videos of little kids getting muddy and being kids, and then throw in baby rabbits.

Want to know what this mother of three is doing with her spare time? Here's what she told me, "I'm in the process of recording some podcasts with a mentor of mine. It stemmed largely out of this generation gap. I hear young mothers constantly in need of wisdom and instruction, so many open and eager to learn from those who have walked before us but unable to find women willing to walk out Titus 2." Keri is using the spare time she has to help young Millennial mothers around her, letting them know they are not alone. She desires older mentors because they have the experience and wisdom. Not only that, she also wants more people around her to have access to the same wisdom.

This cannot be overstated: we need your help. Millennials as a generation are struggling with anxiety, perfectionism, and feeling alone. All of this because they don't see any other way. Share your stories with them. Your experiences are important. You have lived through these same feelings. Being new to a job, failing on a big project, working through that failure, feeling alone. Be a community for them. Let them know they are not on an island. Remind them that their experiences are not some new form of human living but are simply the life stages of growing up. Let them know it is okay to be ordinary; in fact, there is joy found in the everyday.

Point them to Jesus. If you know they are Christian, especially if they go to your church, point them back to the identity they have in Christ. Remind them that no matter what the world throws at them Jesus has claimed them, and they can be secure as His children. Lean heavily into our beautiful sacramental theology of Baptism. Point back to it. Proclaim that in Jesus they are never alone and the Body of Christ is part of their inheritance.

Investing

Proclaiming the truth of Jesus to those outside the Church takes investment, relationship-building, and knowing your story. Don't think that you can walk up to a struggling Millennial and simply ask whether they know where they're going if they die tonight. You have just shut down any chance of connecting with them. Instead, seek out the Millennial God puts in your way and invest in them with your time, your talent, and a bit of your treasure. Think of a Millennial you know. Is he or she a co-worker, a family member, a neighbor? Show them you care. Millennials have grown up with a marketing culture that has sold them everything from bubblegum to cars. They can tell when you are trying to sell them something. Instead, invest in them. This could be as simple as what we like to call the "Snack Guy" principle. No one is going to be upset with someone who brings them a snack, a coffee, or a soda. Invest your time in talking and listening to who they are and why they are struggling. Invest your talent, teach them what you know, pass on your wisdom. Invest your treasure; that coffee ain't going to buy itself. But why do these things for that punk kid next door? Because you care for them. Because the kingdom of heaven is big enough for them. Because Jesus tells you to, and following Him leads to our joy.

Relationship is key. You aren't in it just to gain something. You are investing because you care that Millennials are more than a stereotype—they are people. Let them into your life. Show them the hope you have in Jesus, how it plays out in daily living. Let them see you fail. Let them see you repent and ask for forgiveness. Let them see you accept forgiveness. Get to know them for the sake of getting to know them! Not because you are trying simply to win at the game of getting another Millennial to go to church. Be their friend.

Sharing Your Story

Knowing your story is key to witnessing to Millennials, in fact to all people. Revelation 12:11 tell us, "They [the saints] have conquered him [the devil] by the blood of the Lamb and by the word of their testimony, for they loved not their lives even unto death." Know your testimony, the story of Jesus in your life. Here are a few keys to this:

Know the Main Character—You are a key part of your testimony to be sure, but this is the story of JESUS in your life. Keep the main character the main character.

Ordinary and Extraordinary—Some of you will have extraordinary stories of how Jesus has worked in your life, saving you from immense evils. Some of you will view your story as ordinary and ask, "Why should I even tell it?" Remember, we have all sinned and fallen short of the glory of God; Jesus saves us. The story is not about ordinary versus extraordinary; it is about a Savior who comes for all people.

Justification vs. Sanctification—You are justified by the work of Jesus on the cross. In that act, He who knew no sin became sin for you, rebuilding your relationship with God. As you tell your story, make sure that you let people know there was nothing you could do to earn this gift. But God keeps giving. Sanctification is the process by which we grow as we continue to follow God's way. This is a process. It doesn't gain you salvation but instead flows from it. Make sure to mention how God is at work sanctifying your life, how following Him is the source of your joy. This joy can include happiness, but it is not solely happiness. Joy from God is present in sorrow as much as it is in happiness. This is a joy that surpasses our human understanding.

You Are Not Entitled to Salvation—This fits so well with this chapter. Get excited. Get pumped. Get rowdy. Get **Lit**. God. Saved. You. You didn't deserve it, but He still did it! When you tell your story, share this amazing fact!

Practice telling your story. Write it down and share it with a trusted brother or sister in Christ. Bring it back to the Word, learn more and more what it means to tell your story of Jesus in your life. Then, and I can't stress this enough, share that story. Share it with the Millennial who doesn't know our Savior. Let them see what He has done and is doing for you. Share it with the Millennial from church; let it encourage them in the faith. Really, share it with anyone who will listen! Boomer, Gen Xer, Millennial, and whatever they're calling the kids these days. SHARE THE STORY OF THE GREATEST HOPE YOU HAVE IN YOU!

Investment, relationship, and your story are incredible ways for you to fight the problem of Millennial anxiety. Show them there are people who care. Tell them of the Savior who cares. Now, as we have stated again and again, this is not a book of silver bullets to fix your church's Millennial problem. This all sounds very simple, but it is hard to carry out. Please let us encourage you in your work of connecting to Millennials. It may be a week before you see a connection and an opportunity. It could be a year. But put in the time. Trust that God is working. Fight discouragement and apathy with the truths of Jesus.

You have an incredible opportunity to offer Millennials hope. This generation is stuck in depression and anxiety, and you can share with them all that you have experienced. You can share with them the stories of your younger days. Your wisdom will bless the next generation of workers, neighbors, parents, and churches. Don't let Millennials think they are on an island alone, that no one feels or has felt the way they do. Tell them the story of Jesus in your life and what it means for them!

Where you have the ability, plug in Millennials. Plug them in at your church, at work, in your neighborhood, or any place you have influence. Let them lead and serve. Give them opportunities to fail. Give them opportunities to bless. Watch what they do with the opportunities! Invite them into your service in the neighborhoods and homes of their communities, whether with your church or on your own. Do justice, love mercy, walk humbly, and bring them along for the ride!

In the end, we all struggle with entitlement and are learning to take to heart the last words of Martin Luther, "We are all beggars. This is true."

DISCUSSION QUESTIONS

1. What are things to which you think you are entitled? Why do you feel you're entitled to them?

2. Think back to a time when you failed. What did you learn from the experience?

3. What is the difference between trying to sell someone something and investment?

4. Are there Millennials you can invest in and build relationships with? Who are they? What is your connection to them?

    Chelsey and I find the easiest way to make something happen is to make a simple plan. What is your simple plan for investing in a Millennial?

    Millennials: What is a simple way for you to invest in your church and neighborhood?

DO IT

Take time to pray and ask that the Lord of Life would step in to tear down the anxiety and depression faced by this generation.

Homework: *Write out your testimony. Remember these points: who the main character is, ordinary and extraordinary, justification versus sanctification, and that you are not entitled to salvation.*

OVERLY SENSITIVE

Chelsey

The great irony of this chapter is that it might be interpreted as an offended Millennial writing about how we're not so easily offended. Ah, well.

It is, of course, one of the most common criticisms of this generation: we are too sensitive. We take offense too easily. We require "safe spaces" and "trigger warnings," and we can't disagree agreeably.

And while all of that may be true, I am quite certain sensitivity is not a uniquely Millennial trait. Did you see the American public during the last election cycle? Talk about sour, offended grapes on all sides, of all ages.

To be honest, I think this is one generational trait to which I do not personally relate. I spoke about this to my peers at length, comparing our childhoods, and found that my parents (who are Baby Boomers, but just barely—they would have been Generation X if they had been born just a couple of years later) did not raise me to believe I was any more special or set apart than the next kid. I started babysitting for pocket money at age 11 and haven't gone more than a month without a job or two since. I am the product of a public school education, growing and learning with people who ate free and reduced lunches, who did not speak English as their native language, and who were not Christian. In fact, some were anti-Christian, and they were among my closest friends. (But that's a conversation for another time.)

AN EXAMPLE

I was not a coddled or sheltered child. In fact, I have a very clear memory of sitting on my bed, crying and telling my mom that I didn't want to play freshman volleyball any longer because I thought my coach was being too hard on me.

"Can I quit?" I asked. She sat down with me and shook her head.

"When the season is over, if you feel the same way you do now, you may quit," she said. "But you made a commitment, and that means you stick to your word. But I don't think Coach Abernathy is picking on you. She's trying to help you become a better athlete."

"She's really mean, Mom."

"Maybe so. But you will meet more mean people in life, and you have to learn how to work with them."

"That sucks."

"It's not fun, yes. And don't use that word. Now, I'm going to go make dinner. Why don't you read a book or go for a run? That always makes you feel better."

I told one of my teacher friends about this recently, and she laughed so hard in incredulity that she nearly choked. Apparently, this kind of parental reaction these days is rarer than a hen's tooth.

"She actually told you to go run it off?" she asked, trying to catch her breath.

I shrugged.

"Well, yeah. I did that a lot, whenever I was stressed or angry."

"That would never happen today," said my friend. "If I come down too hard on a student, I get an irate email asking me what exactly my problem is or why I'm bullying their kid—and probably a slap on the wrist from my principal too. I'm just trying to get their kid to do their homework."

"Did your parents ever act like that on your behalf?"

"Oh, yes. My mom used to tell me all the time how much prettier I was than other girls, how much better I was than them, and that the coaches were stupid not to pick me for the dance team, that kind of thing."

"Seriously?"

"Yeah. I mean, I knew she was just doing it to make me feel better. But she did say it a lot."

ONE MORE FOR GOOD MEASURE

One of the most vivid memories I have from my college years is sitting in my freshman Old Testament class, reviewing the syllabus at the beginning of the semester. My professor fixed us with a stern look over his eyeglasses and said that in no uncertain terms would he be taking any calls from our parents about the grades he gave us.

"I had to endure ten minutes of whining from the mother of a student last semester because her son did not think that studying for his final was worthy of his time or effort. If I give you a 50 in this class, you may rest assured: you earned that 50, and no amount of threats or complaints from your helicopter families will change my mind," he told us.

This was not something new in our college experience. Every so often we were in a class where a professor would make this stern proclamation *after* someone's mom had called and dressed him or her down for the test grade her child had received on a test. Those were always fun days to sit in class.

But this was a strange new occurrence for us. Both Ted and I went to public schools. If it was a day late, you got a 50. Two days late was a zero. No questions asked. Many of our friends had the same experience. However, the phenomenon of the helicopter parent was perfected on our Millennial college friends. At the university we attended, there was a point at the end of orientation where parents were taken to one seminar and students to another. Students played games, got to know their fellow freshmen, and some kind of food was involved. Parents, however, were told about the deep care the university had for their kids. How much they knew the trust that had been placed in them. Then parents were asked to head on home so that their students could start getting used to college life.

Some parents left right away. But many ignored this advice, instead opting to hover a little while longer over their kids.

THE SNOWFLAKE GENERATION

You have more than likely heard the term *snowflake* used thus: "Aw, these precious little snowflakes can't handle real life."

The nickname is derived from the fact that no two snowflakes are the same (thereby giving children an inflated sense of their own uniqueness), and they melt easily in the slightest heat (referring to a generation of people who cannot remain cool and calm under stress when presented with opinions differing from their own).

The usage of the term might originate from the novel and later, movie, *Fight Club*, in which someone is told they are not special, they are not a snowflake. Chuck Palahniuk, the author of the original novel, claimed credit for creating the term, adding that the Millennial generation is on the apex of a new wave of Victorianism or, in other terms, a generation of people who cannot handle criticism or critique and therefore look down upon anything with which they do not agree.

The term *Snowflake Generation* was one of *Collins Dictionary*'s words of the year for 2016. They defined it as "the young adults of the 2010s, viewed as being less resilient and more prone to taking offence than previous generations."[xii] Additionally, the *Financial Times* included *snowflake* in their annual Year in a Word list, saying it was a derogatory term for someone who was too emotionally vulnerable to deal with worldviews contrary to their own. This term especially focused on areas, such as universities, where debate used to be a prized commodity. The *Times* went on to note that the insult had become culturally synonymous with Millennials.[xiii]

Pundits pontificate on this topic ad nauseam on cable news, websites, and blogs. The consensus seems to be that parents, in wanting good for their children, protected them from as many forms of dissent, disappointment, and differing opinions that they could. This has created a generation who is distressed by anything that runs contrary to their worldview. When this protection is coupled with entitlement and a call to perfection, it creates an explosive mix.

When overwhelmed by differing worldviews with which they've never had to deal before, some Millennials are prone to overreact with intolerance. This has all contributed to a phenomenon called *no-platforming*, in which presentations, discussions, and debates on controversial topics are no longer allowed on university campuses.

At the University of Oxford, some professors began using trigger warnings to alert students to potentially distressing topics. A trigger warning might be as simple as "viewer discretion advised" prior to a television show, or may be as outrageous as college professors not allowing differing viewpoints to be shared for fear that doing so would harm someone's feelings. Writers heavily criticized this practice, questioning how students hoping to become lawyers could become effective in their careers if they could not even handle a class discussion that may offend them.[xiv]

Is This a Fair Stereotype?

In previous chapters, we have asked this same question: Is this stereotype fair? Does it actually speak the truth about an entire generation? Maybe the better question would be is any stereotype fair? Are stereotypes of older generations fair? The point is that no stereotype can be fair. It is an overgeneralization. It is built to try to classify a group as a whole instead of getting to know its individual parts. The human tendency is to stereotype. It is easier to stereotype a person who disagrees with you than to try to connect with them. Looking past these overgeneralizations, one can see the person instead of the statistics and assumptions.

Oversensitivity points to a deeper human issue: the human tendency to seek comfort over all things. This is an idol among idols. Seeking our own needs above all others enables us to live in a sheltered place where our comfort becomes our chief concern. This is the reason for oversensitivity. It is a need to remain comfortable at all costs.

To be sure, some (perhaps even a majority of Millennials) struggle with feeling threatened by differing opinions, criticism from harsh superiors, and even seem unable to conduct polite discourse. When walking into a world full of divergent opinions, the assault on a strongly held worldview can seem antagonistic. We all struggle with oversensitivity on certain topics. Maybe, just maybe, this is an issue about where humans find their identity rather than a generational sin.

ECHO CHAMBERS AND FAKE NEWS

At times, it is a struggle to hold your tongue on social media. This truism seems to multiply tenfold during election season. More often than not, if a Facebook friend posts something we find offensive, it is easy to make liberal use of the "mute" button so we no longer have to see their posts in our news feeds. Sometimes, we might go so far as unfriending them—not because we hate them, but because we don't trust ourselves not to shoot our mouths off in a snarky comment. Please pay attention to this next detail.

Are you paying attention?

It is not worth losing a real, flesh-and-blood friendship over a difference in opinion that was expressed online without body language or tone of voice.

I am going to repeat that one more time.

It is not worth losing a real, flesh-and-blood friendship over a difference in opinion that was expressed online without body language or tone of voice.

You have to be able to gauge what is worth tuning out for the sake of friendship and what is simply about your own comfort level. If you tune out and mute all voices that are not like your own, what you have created is an echo chamber. We may often label this as taking care of ourselves, avoiding a vicious and never-ending news cycle. But what happens when we do this so the only voices we hear are the ones with which we agree?

Millennials are not the only ones to fall into such a trap. This is a cross-generational sin: people of all ages like to bolster their perspectives with like-minded information.

When we listen to only the voices like our own, we easily allow ourselves to fall for news that does not offer any differing viewpoints. Some may label this fake news. But this issue starts with our desire to see only things that make us feel more comfortable. While Millennials may be blamed for being snowflakes, it is a human trait to seek out only the things that bring us comfort. As Christians, we have a Savior who comforts us, but we are not called to a life of comfort. Jesus actually promises us hardship. He tells us, "I have said these things to you, that in Me you may have peace. In the world you will have tribulation. But take heart; I have overcome the world" (John 16:33).

We should not fear other viewpoints. If we know that the truth is Jesus, then what do we have to fear?

Confirmation bias, or the tendency to interpret new information as confirmation of one's existing beliefs or theories, is nothing new.

So, What Can Be Done?

The media has a lot to do with the development of online echo chambers. I have a friend (a Millennial) whose favorite online pastime is checking to see if the news articles posted on his social media feeds are in fact truthful. If they aren't, he posts a link disproving or clarifying the article in the comments.

It is truly alarming how often the original poster deletes my friend's comments. We don't like to admit when we are wrong or when we fall in with false information.

(Even worse is when someone posts a satirical article, written by a site like **The Onion** or **The Babylon Bee**, as fact. NOTE: These are joke websites. The things they post are generally completely untrue, written for entertainment value. Please be a responsible consumer of information and double-check whether the latest piece of "news" that outrages you is, in fact, a joke.)

According to the Pew Research Center, 62 percent of American adults received their news through social media in 2016[xv]—and these were adults of all ages. But maybe you don't see Millennials engaging at the same rate on your Facebook page. That's not because we have become more enlightened or even kinder. We have simply moved on to more abbreviated forms of social media like Twitter and Snapchat. Now you can get our anger in 140 characters or less.

The inclination to promote one's preferred beliefs is natural (one of the first things we learn as infants is to categorize things into schemas, after all), but too much personal confirmation bias creates gaps, which can lead to demonizing others. This is detrimental to producing a democratic society, of course, but it is downright shameful within the Body of Christ.

Much has been written about irresponsible media and the need for holding our news sources to higher standards, but we're uncertain whether such standards will ever be raised in an age of an ever-increasing demand for immediate information, instant gratification, and constant entertainment.

The good news is that even more immediate steps to rectify this problem are simple and can start with you. It looks like this: intentionally talk to, get to know, and follow (on social media, anyway) people with whom you disagree.

For me, this is has looked like personally going to some friends of mine and apologizing for unfriending them on social media in the first place. It has looked like holding my tongue online and asking the person to have a coffee with me so we can have a discussion face-to-face. It has looked like reminding myself to separate the person from what they say online and who they actually are. And it has looked like purposefully reading, listening to, and surrounding myself with people who are different from me. After all, differences of opinion make for well-rounded, well-informed citizens, and knowing the stories of the other creates empathy, a helpful quality one could employ while spreading the Gospel.

FREE LISTENING

My brother-in-law, Andrew, is a very smart guy. I have not confirmed this with him, but I think he saw me falling into the echo chamber I was creating for myself online, and he proceeded to very tactfully convict me of this. Or maybe he just thought I would like it because I am so self-aware. My ego would like to go with that reason, so we'll leave things there and continue.

He sent me a blog post by a man named Benjamin Mathes. Mathes is not a Republican (though to which political party he belongs, I am not sure), but he went to the 2016 Republican National Convention and stood outside the meeting, holding up a sign that read "Free Listening."

In the post, Mathes described how most people who saw the sign that day spoke to him about surface-level things, such as where they were from, their families, and what they did for a living. One woman, however, walked toward him with a very determined look on her face and announced that she thought abortion was an act of murder.

Now, of course, as Christians and those who seek to build the kingdom of God on earth, we agree with this woman. But the writer, Mathes, did not. He continued, explaining that as she began to expound upon her statement, he felt the old familiar boiling in his stomach; he yearned to interrupt her and tell her his story. He naturally wanted to begin arguing.

But he didn't. Instead, he listened until she stopped speaking, and then said: "Thank you for sharing that. Tell me your story. I'd love to know how you came to this point of view."

The woman was taken aback.

"Why? The sign just says 'Free Listening,' so I gave you something to listen to."

"Give me more to listen to," said Mathes, and so she did.

Her dearest desire had always been to become a mother, but she was just eighteen when she found out she could not have children. She kept it a secret from her husband later on, who left her after he found out. She called herself old, and asked Mathes: "Who will ever love me now?"[xvi]

Mathes wrote that his heart broke, and he realized in that moment that sometimes (in fact, most times), the debate isn't about the debate. The debate is about the people.

This is how Christians ought to be approaching one another. Not with weapons, but with patience, empathy, love, and the peace that only Christ can offer a broken and hurting world. It is hard work. As Christians, we have to overcome the prejudices that have wormed their way into our hearts, those things of the flesh that seek self over honoring others. That is why it is important to get to know people as opposed to ideas.

Not every conversation you have will feel fruitful. Mathes and the woman left each other that day with the same opinions they brought with them. And that's okay, because Peter wrote to the Corinthians about such strife and division: "So neither he who plants nor he who waters is anything, but only God who gives the growth" (1 Corinthians 3:6).

Make yourself available for conversation. Listen. Learn. Pray—either right there with that person, if you feel so led, or afterward. Extend peace and truth in love, and rest in the truth that God will give the growth.

What's more—you, Christian, have nothing to fear from differences of opinion. Did you know that? I hope so. It's a fact I often forget, due to my tendency to forget my identity as a redeemed child of God.

SLAYING OUR IDOLS

Why do we go to church every Sunday? Why not once a month? Why not a couple of times a year? There are many answers to this question, and we could write an entire book on them. But one major reason is that our God is in the business of slaying our idols.

As we've discussed, oversensitivity comes from seeking the idol of comfort. We are told to have no idols. It's a commandment. You can look it up (Exodus 20:3). The idol of comfort did not suddenly appear when Millennials were born. It is an idol that has persisted since the fall in the garden. It is easy for any generation to look at another and say, "Look at your issues! You just need to do what we tell you to do and like it!"

Are there Millennials who are overly sensitive? Yes. But know there is a large group of Millennials who are just as frustrated with their generational peers in this area as you are. However, let's take a step back.

Millennials. Gen Xers. Boomers.

Where have you sought comfort rather than God's commands? When have you placed this idol over loving and trusting God? Growing in our faith means we must repent of these kinds of things. It's not easy. But it will lead to our joy.

That is the process of sanctification at work—God taking away those sinful behaviors, those idols that lead us away from Him. It feels to our sinful selves as if we are losing a piece of who we are, but in fact, we are being re-created into what God had originally envisioned for us.

What if instead of looking at other generations with anger about their sensitivities, we could have conversations where empathy ruled the day? In Jesus' day, a Roman solider on a march could stop anyone along the road and force them to carry his gear for a mile. Could you imagine? You're out walking your dog, enjoying the day, when an armed man stops you and forces you to carry his heavy pack! Of course, Jesus' response to this practice is incredible: "and if anyone forces you to go one mile, go with him two miles" (Matthew 5:41).

There are few people, if any, with whom you have as large a grievance as the Jewish people of biblical Jerusalem had with Roman soldiers. Rome had a simple solution for holding their vast empire and far-reaching territories: force the population to pay for their occupying force and put down any rebellion with ruthless brutality. Why were tax collectors so hated in New Testament times? These were men who had sold out their fellow countrymen to help fund the army that would crucify their families, friends, and neighbors to show their authority.

But Jesus calls His followers to go the extra mile. Why? Because He came to save those very Roman soldiers. His goal was not just to save the Jewish people; it was the whole world. He knew that going two miles with a Roman solider would catch their attention because it is against the way the world works. When someone is against you, you are against them.

Does your need to express your own views create an echo chamber where you cannot hear out the Millennials in your life? Have you set yourself up so that you hear only what you agree with?

MILLENNIALS, QUICK SIDEBAR . . .

Does your need to express your own worldview create an echo chamber where you cannot hear out the older generations in your life? Have you set yourself up so that you hear only what you agree with? Hearing out those who hold differing viewpoints is hard, often because we are preparing to return fire as soon as they are done. My father-in-law puts it this way: imagine a conversation like Ping-Pong. All you're trying to do is return the volley with as much speed and force as you can. This type of conversation looks heated, intense, and shows little care or empathy for the other person, only your need to win. Now imagine instead of a Ping-Pong paddle you had a net. The person across from you fires a volley your way. Instead of swinging away, you catch the ball in the net, pull it out, take a look at it, and toss it back. You haven't escalated the situation. Instead, you've slowed down the game, asked some questions, and tried to understand the other person's point of view.

As the Church, we must be leaders in the process of dismantling echo chambers. If we begin to draw lines against one another, the enemy has won. Instead of being the group that yells the loudest at the others, may we be a place where we can come together and walk the extra mile with one another. Watch how the Millennial generation reacts to that.

IDENTITY IN CHRIST

We, as members of the Body of Christ, have an unshakable and blessed assurance: There is one way to the Father, and it is through Jesus, His Son. We are His children through His death and resurrection. This saving work is given to us as a gift, and "neither death nor life, nor angels nor rulers, nor things present nor things to come, nor powers, nor height nor depth, nor anything else in all creation, will be able to separate us from the love of God in Christ Jesus our Lord" (Romans 8:38–39).

I would like to venture an educated guess and say that many people (ourselves included) lash out intolerantly against those with whom we disagree because we forget this truth. When we fear our self-worth is on the line, our tongues become more barbed, our thoughts become unkind. When we feel threatened, we threaten back. Such unpleasantness is unnecessary and detrimental to productive discussion. More important, it also builds dividing walls within the Body of Christ. And if you think this is nothing new—you're right.

I can only imagine how deeply entrenched were the obstacles that the Early Church had to overcome. We read about many obstacles to unity in the Epistles.

One of the biggest divisions in the New Testament was that between Jew and Gentile. The Jewish people were God's chosen people; from them would come the Savior. Gentiles were those on the outside. However, we are told:

> Therefore remember that at one time you Gentiles in the flesh, called "the uncircumcision" by what is called the circumcision, which is made in the flesh by hands—remember that you were at that time separated from Christ, alienated from the commonwealth of Israel and strangers to the covenants of the promise, having no hope and without God

in the world. But now in Christ Jesus you who once were far off have been brought near by the blood of Christ. For He Himself is our peace, who has made us both one and has broken down in His flesh the dividing wall of hostility by abolishing the law of commandments expressed in ordinances, that He might create in Himself one new man in place of the two, so making peace, and might reconcile us both to God in one body through the cross, thereby killing the hostility. (Ephesians 2:11–16)

Paul speaks here to those who have until this point in history been known as the foreigner—the other—those pagans who are not the children of Israel. The Jews must have been at least a *little* angry about this, if not furious in some cases.

This is also why the parable of the workers in the vineyard in the Book of Matthew has always rankled me, a lifelong Christian, a little bit. My linear view of life, my sense of self-importance and of the "sacrifices" I have made to follow God's commandments tell me that I ought to expect to be set apart at least a *little* bit from the thief on the cross.

And yet, my works are nothing more than smoke on a very swift wind—here today, gone tomorrow, and created in advance for me by my heavenly Father to do.

Oversensitivity is one of the hardest issues to deal with when it comes to the Millennial generation. Simply telling us we are oversensitive elicits a reaction because we are sensitive to that kind of criticism. Here is the ask: please be patient with us. Instead of reacting to our oversensitivity with offense, look to see if you can walk the extra mile, to see the root of the issue instead of becoming distracted by our gut reaction.

Remember, this is a sin issue; we will also try to remember that we need to be aware of this when we live in our own echo chambers. But as the Church, together, we need to tackle the idol of personal comfort. It is one of our greatest joys to watch as the Lord lays down our idols, grinding them into dust. All we need to do is repent and walk in new life.

MILLENNIALS, CAN WE ENCOURAGE YOU FOR A MINUTE?

The world is trying, constantly, to answer for you the question "Where does my identity find its foundation?" And this is happening at an alarming rate. This isn't new. The problem is the speed at which we are inundated with those idols that want to take the pivotal role in our identities. Hear this: you are loved. You are worthwhile. Nothing that you can say or do can separate you from the love God has for you that is found in Jesus. God isn't waiting for a better version of you to somehow love you more. He loves you as who you are now. Oftentimes, we struggle with being "snowflakes" because of our insecurity in the identity we have in Jesus. Run to Him. Return to Him. A while back, Ted taught on the parable of the prodigal son during worship. The story hit him in a new way this time around. He was struck by the fact that the father comes out to meet both of his sons. In response to the younger son, who has gone off and lived a wild lifestyle, the father races to meet him on the road. With the older son, who is moping outside of the party, the father comes out to meet him. When our identities are found somewhere else, when we put our foundations on idols, remember this: God our Father is looking to come out and meet us, to remind us that we are His children. We already have His love.

But as a favorite seminary professor often remarked, what does this mean for me on Monday? Enter conversations with your identity firmly rooted in Jesus. You do not need to lash out because He has already claimed you. Surround yourself with differing voices. Not so that you follow all of them, but so that you are aware of them. Once again, your identity is in Jesus, and He will keep you anchored to Him.

Oversensitivity is driven by a need to find comfort. Let us seek to be comforted by our Savior, not to seek to be comfortable.

DISCUSSION QUESTIONS

1. What are some topics you become oversensitive about? Why do you think that is?

2. How can we as the Church be countercultural to the ideas of comfort and snowflake-ness?

3. Where is Jesus calling you to walk the extra mile?

4. In John 15:5, Jesus tells us, "I am the vine; you are the branches. Whoever abides in Me and I in him, he it is that bears much fruit, for apart from Me you can do nothing." Abiding in Jesus is core to keeping our identity rooted in Him. What are some ways that you can think of to abide in the Lord?

DO IT

All Generations: *Find someone from another generation with whom you might disagree. Have dinner with them. Can't do dinner? Grab a beer. Don't like beer? Grab a coffee. The point? Spend time with them. Pray that the Lord would help you walk that extra mile, would shatter your echo chambers, and crush the idol of comfort under His feet.*

5

US VS. THEM

Ted

Y ou did it! You made it through the stereotypes. We're proud of you. Here's a trophy.

Just kidding. You only participated. No trophy for you. Come and talk to me when you win a championship.[5]

But you have made it through the main stereotypes of my generation, the ideas that pervade through our culture about what makes a Millennial . . . a Millennial. Sitting and writing this chapter, I have heard and read several accounts that once again place blame for what is happening around us solely on Millennials: cultural breakdown, shrinking church attendance, and self-centered ways of life, to name a few. Some of this is fair criticism. Some of it is basic stereotyping. But when we drill down, what is the real issue here?

I propose that the answer is our love for a fight. To sit on the right side of an argument. To ignore our own issues and point out those of others.

---

5   This joke is funny because of participation trophies.

The temptation to make our generational differences an Us vs. Them battle.

This is not some single generational issue either. There are no right sides in this battle. My generation is quick to push all kinds of blame away from ourselves. It is much easier to blame a system, our parents, or the generations before us than it is to take ownership of our issues. In my own weakness, I have shaken my head and muttered "Boomers" under my breath in frustrated exasperation.

Let us, Chelsey and me, then be the first to apologize for the times Millennials have reacted poorly. In our frustration, we have made you, Boomer or Xer, the problem. With a flippant attitude and an air of hipster superiority, we pass the problems the Church faces onto the older generations. It is easier for us to blame your ideas, penchants, and stereotypes instead of owning the heartbreaking fact that so many of our friends have left the faith. It is an easy move to say that there are no Millennials in the Church when we drive straight home from work and don't engage our neighbors with the Gospel. Please forgive us when we have been rude or self-righteous in our views instead of hearing your wisdom. Our battle is not against you.

In the same breath, please recognize your battle is not against us. It is against the powers and principalities of the spiritual realm. The devil would have you believe that our culture, our nation, and our churches are falling apart because of the young people. He seeks to distract you, to focus your frustration on the flesh and blood of the people in front of you instead of recognizing how his power plays for the heart of a generation. Because that is the fight. Millennials are leaving the Church. The statistics on how many are leaving and how quickly they are leaving the Church vary, but none of the statistics are good. If we can be distracted into frustration with other members of Christ's Church, then we lose sight of the goal: more Millennials in the kingdom of God. That is what our enemy fears, that young people would return to God, that their hearts would be convicted and turned by the power of the Holy Spirit. If the battle between Millennials and older generations rages inside the Church, then it is not waged for the hearts of those far away from the Lord.

All of this sounds like rhetoric . . . partially because it is . . . but it is so much more than that.

THE FALSE BATTLE

The battle belongs to the Lord. A simple but true phrase. We do not fear who will win the fight at the end of the day, but let's make sure we are in the right fight! As the Church Militant—the Church on earth that lives in a broken world—we are invited into the battle. Our job is not to destroy the people around us, but instead to declare the Kingdom that is to come. Conviction and repentance are a part of that plan, but so are kindness, gentleness, peace, patience, and goodness. The identity of the Church as the people of God on earth must remain rooted in Jesus' death for our sins and His resurrection for our new life.

On June 6, 1944, the Allies launched the largest invasion known to man against Hitler's forces in Europe. The plan was to attack along the western coastline of France in Normandy. But the narrowest point of crossing on the English Channel is on the northern portion of the west coast of France at Pas-de-Calais. It was here that the Third Reich concentrated a majority of their defenses. To make sure that more troops, armor, and supplies were focused away from the main battle, the Allies conceived a brilliant plan: Operation Fortitude. Using plywood, inflatables, old boats, and a massive system of tents, they built a fake staging ground for an invasion. The Allies sold this as much as they could. For every bomb dropped in Normandy, more were dropped near Calais. They set up fake radio messages, had men running around as if they were going about the business of an invasion, and placed the best-known general in the US Army, General George S. Patton, in the midst of this camp. They sold the invasion of Calais. When the combined forces of the Allies landed in Normandy on June 6, much-needed man and machine power was left to sit in Calais because Axis leaders believed the Normandy landing was a feint for the real invasion that would come to the north. If you ever want to see something surreal, Google "inflatable tank ww2" and check out some of the images and videos!

Deception is one of the oldest strategies of warfare. The Allies were the good guys, but how much more will someone who is evil use deception to their advantage? Our enemy is a skilled craftsman of deception. Here, the devil deceives us into believing that our battle rages between generations, that the old is better than the new, or that the elders have ruined everything for their children. It is easy to fall into the deception. Let us not be deceived.

Let me tell you clearly: Millennials are not the enemy. Will you struggle with them? Yes. Are there generational differences? A canyon's worth. Are there reasons for the believable stereotypes? As a Millennial, even I see Millennial stereotypes rear their ugly heads. Yet Millennials are not the enemy.

MILLENNIALS, HEAR ME CLEARLY . . .

Older generations are not the enemy. Will you struggle with them? Yes. Are there generational differences? A canyon's worth. Will they continue to post articles, blogs, political statements, and videos that blame you for the downfall of society? Yep. Yet older generations are not the enemy.

The enemy is the deceiver who would have us believe that we are at war with one another. Remember this verse from earlier in this book: "One generation shall commend your works to another, and shall declare your mighty acts" (Psalm 145:4). There is power in one generation passing down the ways of the faith to the next. The devil is seeking to destroy that very power. Scripture tells us over and over that *the* way discipleship and growth happens as we follow Jesus is through imitation. Paul tells us, "Be imitators of me, as I am of Christ" (1 Corinthians 11:1).

This is *the* way the faith is passed on from one generation to the next. The Holy Spirit brings faith and works through older generations to work with and mentor those growing in their faith. If the devil can cast the focus of the Church from this task to a generational dispute, he gains a foothold in the battle for the hearts of all generations. Do not be deceived. Our battle is not Millennials vs. Boomers, Gen Xers vs. Millennials, or even Gen Xers vs. Boomers, or anything in between. Our battle is with the very forces of darkness that seek to lead people away from the knowledge that Jesus is for them, that He has come, and there is salvation through Him.

LEARNING TO LAMENT

If we can truly identify the battle, then what are we supposed to do next? One of the first things the Church can do is embrace and learn better the practice of lamenting.

I lead a college-age Bible study with some folks from our church. One night over Torchy's Tacos,[6] I asked them a simple question, "What do you look for in a church?" The maturity displayed was incredible. Their answers were simple: community, preaching that reminds me of my sin but proclaims Jesus for me, authenticity, and a place that welcomes new people. These were all impressive answers, and we had some great discussion around them. But there was one answer that stuck out to me. One of our guys thought deeply and then said, "I don't want my church to always be happy." Intrigued, I asked him what he meant. He replied that he wanted to be involved in a church that was able to see that people aren't happy all the time. In this moment, he shared how in his life he isn't always in a happy place, and he finds comfort when the Church acknowledges that unhappiness occurs in life, but Jesus is still greater. He wanted the Church to be able to lament.

---

6   If you are ever in Austin, do yourself a favor . . . get Torchy's Tacos!

> **What is lamenting? It is acknowledging the realities of our world while still trusting in the hope of Jesus.**

What is lamenting? It is acknowledging the realities of our world while still trusting in the hope of Jesus. The Bible is full of lamenting; the whole Book of Lamentations is devoted to it. Throughout Scripture, we find examples of things going wrong but people still trusting God. The Book of Psalms has beautifully poetic laments. The prophets often lament as Israel turns from the ways of the Lord. Job is full of lament over the loss of his entire livelihood, family, and possessions. Paul and Peter constantly lament the ways of the world in their letters to the Early Church, but they continually point back to the hope found in Christ. Look at these powerful laments from Scripture:

> Oh, grant us help against the foe, for vain is the salvation of man! With God we shall do valiantly; it is He who will tread down our foes. (Psalm 60:11–12)

> Turn again, O God of hosts! Look down from heaven, and see; have regard for this vine, the stock that Your right hand planted, and for the son whom You made strong for Yourself. They have burned it with fire; they have cut it down; may they perish at the rebuke of Your face! But let Your hand be on the man of Your right hand, the son of man whom You have made strong for Yourself! Then we shall not turn back from You; give us life, and we will call upon Your name! Restore us, O LORD God of hosts! Let Your face shine, that we may be saved! (Psalm 80:14–19)

> For I know that my Redeemer lives, and at the last He will stand upon the earth. (Job 19:25)

> I have become the laughingstock of all peoples, the object of their taunts all day long. He has filled me with bitterness; He has sated me with wormwood. He has made my teeth grind on gravel, and made me cower in ashes; my soul is bereft of

peace; I have forgotten what happiness is; so I say, "My endurance has perished; so has my hope from the LORD." Remember my affliction and my wanderings, the wormwood and the gall! My soul continually remembers it and is bowed down within me. But this I call to mind, and therefore I have hope: The steadfast love of the LORD never ceases; His mercies never come to an end; they are new every morning; great is Your faithfulness. "The LORD is my portion," says my soul, "therefore I will hope in Him." (Lamentations 3:14–24)

The saying is trustworthy and deserving of full acceptance, that Christ Jesus came into the world to save sinners, of whom I am the foremost. But I received mercy for this reason, that in me, as the foremost, Jesus Christ might display His perfect patience as an example to those who were to believe in Him for eternal life. To the King of the ages, immortal, invisible, the only God, be honor and glory forever and ever. Amen. (1 Timothy 1:15–17)

Lament is a gift in the life of the disciple. But why do we need it? What is the importance of lamenting in our lives? Why is it so vital to bridging the generational divides?

Lamenting frees us from anxiety surrounding the issues of our world. There are many things in our culture today that seem to be assailing us, yet the call on the Christian person is to not be anxious. Lamenting is a gift from God that gives us the ability to express our concerns, fears, and anxieties with the reality in which we live. Biblical lamentation never pulls any punches. In fact, it is incredibly harsh in its portrayal of the world. But those lamentations always return to the steadfast love of God. While anxiety will always be an issue we struggle with as fallen humans, lamenting gives us the ability to express those things to God while simultaneously remembering the promises we have in Him.

MILLENNIALS . . .

When it comes to the Millennial generation as a whole, we must lament. I say this as a Millennial, so know that I am in the trenches with you. Yet, the stark reality of our generation is that we are not only leaving churches in droves but are in fact leaving the faith. The rise of the nones has been a key story in the media and throughout the American church over the last several years. Let us lament. A young generation is leaving the Church, it has become antagonistic to following Jesus, and wants to be affirmed in anything that leads to "happiness." The great idol of self is destroying communities all the while. "What is best for me . . . " echoes as a mantra throughout coffee shops, bars, podcasts, and blogs. But the God of the universe knows. He sees. And He is a God who seeks those who are lost. He has a burning passion to renew the world to Him. He sent His Son to an ugly and gut-wrenching death so that His creation could once again be restored. While our generation may be leaving Him, He is not leaving us.

Older generations, please hear the lament of Millennials in your church, especially in many of our Lutheran churches. We are alone. We want to seek after the ways of Jesus but all too often are told, "It's not your turn to ___." You can fill in the blank for what that means—it's not your turn to lead, to speak, to serve, and so on. From every angle, we are assailed with commentary describing how our generation is destroying many things it touches. When we are labeled "Millennial," we cringe, because it feels like a curse, and at the same time we want to be proud of who we are. We know we are told not to be looked down upon because of our youth, yet often it feels as if that youth is the millstone around our necks. Our generation is deeply connected to our friends who are far from the Lord, but we trust that He has placed generations ahead of us to help guide us and lead us. We trust that He is not casting us aside but is in fact calling us to the work of His Church.

Let us lament together. Let us walk together to the foot of the cross to share our fears and anxieties with the One who can do something about them, Jesus. This is His promise to us, "I have said these things to you, that in Me you may have peace. In the world you will have tribulation. But take heart; I have overcome the world" (John 16:33).

LEARNING TO LISTEN

Lamenting is the first step to reminding us who the battle is against; learning to listen is another key factor in returning to the battlefield. Listening offers us the chance to see what is happening in the lives of others. Instead of classifying them based on stereotypes or generalities, it lets us see their daily struggles. It facilitates the removal of people from battlefield, allowing us to refocus on the spiritual warfare being waged.

Preparing for this book, I went to some Millennial friends who are leaders in their church and asked them this question: "What would be some things that you would want people to know about what it means to be a Millennial leader in the Church, good or bad?"

Here are some of the responses I received:

> **"** When it comes to church leadership, the challenge centers on trying to lead a congregation that thinks 180 degrees differently than you do. There is an element of having a genuine passion and excitement for Jesus. . . . It is not that previous generations did not have a passion, rather their passion was ingrained, part of their make up, their DNA from day one. For Millennials, it is altogether different. Yes, for many of us it [passion] has become our primary support, hope, and comfort, but for each of us it was a conscious choice at some time to remain in faith. It is not an 'I decided to come to faith,' that was and will always be the work of the Spirit, but it is a very clear 'I have decided to follow Jesus.' Faced with direct challenge and confrontation to our faith, either via conversation or just general

popular perception, we have had to actively choose to profess Jesus."

" *Recently I've had some friends/connections of the Millennial persuasion who have left or are about to leave their current positions [in the Church]. Some away from ministry, some to other positions [within the Church]. What strikes me is often the unwillingness for change or at least to see a situation from another perspective. Here's what I mean. Many of us have been raised to respond to difficulty/challenge/things we don't like by simply changing the situation or leaving. Some of that is a good thing. What's surprising is that the same generation who raised us is now surprised that Millennials are so 'elusive' and don't stay around—whether that be an employer, church, or whatever. So the typical response to the challenge is to ask, 'What's wrong with the Millennials?' as opposed to 'What's wrong/unhealthy about this situation?'"*

These were simple answers to a simple question. All I did was type it into Facebook messenger. In a similar way, I sent this question to some trusted Boomer and Gen X leaders in the church: When it comes to the Millennial generation, what do you find are some of the hardest aspects of leading them in the church?

Here are some responses:

" *Busyness."*

" *Forgetting that discipleship requires time with them."*

" *Parents who rejected . . .Christ or "the church" before them, no mentoring from the home."*

" *Being unsure of what they [Millennials] need and how to deliver it."*

" *I have to love them so much that I want to lead them, I need to not want to just throw my hands up, I need to have a loving passion for them."*

" *Dang. I just want them to come to church and know Jesus.*"

" *We're so bad at reaching and interesting them—unless they're so bought in they are literally giving their whole lives to Jesus.*"

" *I am much older than them so I'm not at a similar life stage. That's hard. I sense they are more strongly influenced by a nonbiblical worldview than previous generations (homosexuality, evolution, etc.).*"

There are important things we all need to hear; the question is, can we listen? Is there room in our churches and lives to sit down, ask the hard questions, and actively listen to the answers? It is important that the older generations in the church hear the Millennials. It is of great importance for Millennials to sit and listen graciously to the wisdom of older generations.

But what will happen if we continue to talk over each other? In researching for this book, we came across many varied sources from Millennials about how someone from an older generation would come to them and tell them all the problems with Millennials. They wouldn't listen to the expert standing right in front of them, an actual Millennial, but instead considered themselves experts on the generation because of a news report. We have also encountered the opposite effect. Millennials tend to blame all their issues on the older generations. The idea goes that if I am _____ as a Millennial, you made me this way because you _____ . Blame is shifted away from our own actions toward others. We don't listen but instead justify why we are the way we are.

What if instead we walked in humility and asked one another hard questions? Listening to, instead of yelling at, one another is a key way to fight the battle against the devil.

Which brings us to . . .

FINDING YOUR SECURITY IN JESUS . . . NOT IN BEING RIGHT

Deep in each of us lies a need to be right. It doesn't matter what it is. Millennials do this at lightning speed because of one thing: Google. No longer do arguments about who played what character in what movie, what the correct form of cooking a dish is, or finding out the greatest second baseman in the history of baseball[7] take a protracted amount of time. These are solved within the milliseconds it takes to pull out a phone and type the question into Google. We all have a deep, innate need to be justified through our rightness.

Yet, when it comes to connecting generations, can we let our need to be right stand to the side for the sake of relationship? Here is what I mean. Go look at social media. At any point during the day there is some form of argument happening on Twitter feeds, Facebook walls, and You-Tube videos. It seems like every day we are hearing about some new feud that started because one person tweeted something that another person took the wrong way and all of a sudden they're off to the races. But here is the more devastating thing: when Christians argue with one another on social media. When instead of showing gentleness, kindness, and love, they attack via snide comments and character assassinations. All because they want to be right.

Please hear me. I am not saying there is not right and wrong. It is good to know that truth will set us free (John 8:32). But what is truth in that passage? The truth is Jesus. When He says that the truth will set those who believe in Him free, it is because of the fact that He must and will be lifted up, that He must go to the cross for them. It is easy for Christians to fall into our old habits of being fickle and foolish and losing sight of the truth in our lives. Instead of seeing Jesus as the foundation of identity, it is easy to build houses on the sandy shores of knowledge, self-righteousness, and piety. The need to be right and justified cannot come from being right on social media. Social media is out in the world for all to see. And

---

7   You don't have to Google this one; it's Craig Biggio.

what are Millennials outside the Church seeing? Christians who cannot control themselves. Christians who lash out against their perceived enemies left and right, as if the God of the universe needs their defense. It is important for us to hold fast to our beliefs. It is important for us to defend our beliefs. But if the Holy Spirit is working in us, two of the fruits we will display are *gentleness* and *kindness*. Millennials look in and see pastors, church workers, and other Christians in their lives lashing out over disagreements.

Let's look at how Scripture speaks of how we are to treat those we view as our enemies:

> But I say to you who hear, Love your enemies, do good to those who hate you. (Luke 6:27)

> Repay no one evil for evil, but give thought to do what is honorable in the sight of all. If possible, so far as it depends on you, live peaceably with all. Beloved, never avenge yourselves, but leave it to the wrath of God, for it is written, "Vengeance is Mine, I will repay, says the Lord." To the contrary, "if your enemy is hungry, feed him; if he is thirsty, give him something to drink; for by so doing you will heap burning coals on his head." Do not be overcome by evil, but overcome evil with good. (Romans 12:17–21)

> You have heard that it was said, "You shall love your neighbor and hate your enemy." But I say to you, Love your enemies and pray for those who persecute you, so that you may be sons of your Father who is in heaven. For He makes His sun rise on the evil and on the good, and sends rain on the just and on the unjust. For if you love those who love you, what reward do you have? Do not even the tax collectors do the same? And if you greet only your brothers, what more are you doing than others? Do not even the Gentiles do the same? You therefore must be perfect, as your heavenly Father is perfect. (Matthew 5:43–48)

> Let all bitterness and wrath and anger and clamor and slander be put away from you, along with all malice. Be kind to one another, tenderhearted, forgiving one another, as God in Christ forgave you. (Ephesians 4:31–32)

> A soft answer turns away wrath, but a harsh word stirs up anger. (Proverbs 15:1)

Can you let it go? Can you say, "I do not need to prove my rightness. . . . Jesus is my truth"? Will you be the Christian leader who seeks to reconcile rather than spit vitriol? Because Millennials are watching.

As Christians, will we fight the wrong battle? That is the great question of this generational gap. Will we believe that our fight is against flesh and blood, or will we see the battle for the heart of a generation? Fighting with one another is complicated but easy. It feels good to be able to speak down to another person, to blame another group of people for your fears and anxieties.

Let us instead be the Church Militant. We do not fight the battles of this earth, but instead seek for the kingdom of God with incredible focus and determination. As Christians, our hearts are with a lost generation instead of against them. We need to listen and ask good questions, instead of feeling threatened by their responses. Our justification comes from God, not from our ability to throw 140-character insults at other people on Twitter.

There is hope. We lament that a generation is wandering farther and farther from the Lord. But we trust in His promise that those who are far off, He will bring near.

Over the next several chapters we will present you with the incredible opportunities you have as the Church, the Body of Christ, and within your local churches to proclaim the works of the Lord to the Millennial generation.

DISCUSSION QUESTIONS

1. What are you lamenting right now in your life? in the life of the Church? What promises of God speak to this lament?

2. Millennials: What are some ways you feel misunderstood by older generations?

3. Older generations: What are some ways you feel misunderstood by Millennials?

4. What are the hard questions you would like to ask Millennials? What are the hard questions you would like to ask the older generations? (Keep these questions from being an attack on one another.)

5. How do you go overboard on social media? How do you think this is viewed by people from the outside looking in?

DO IT

Write a lament. Look at the world, acknowledge the realities around you, don't hold back. Then follow up your lament with the promises of Jesus. What is the hope you have in Him?

PART 2
ENGAGING MILLENNIALS

RELATIONSHIPS

Ted

Besides being Saturday morning cartoons, what do G.I. Joe, the Teenage Mutant Ninja Turtles, and Captain Planet all have in common? They're all trying to sell you something.

At the time when Millennials were waking up to run downstairs and catch the morning block of cartoons, advertisers were already making their way into our young brains. All three of the shows mentioned above taught some form of lesson. G.I. Joe taught us that knowing was half the battle. Ninja Turtles taught us the word *cowabunga* and a deep love for pizza. Captain Planet beamed environmentalism right into our brains.

However, all three of these shows were also working to sell one thing: toys. Action figures. Playsets. Vehicles. Every one of them tried to sell us something that we just *had* to have. From infancy to adulthood, Millennials have been the target of massive marketing campaigns. From movies to Instagram, every product we use seems to offer something else for us to buy. Because of this, Millennials can smell the hard sell a mile away.

The struggle that the Church can fall into is trying to sell Jesus to potential buyers who just aren't all that interested in the product. Everything the Church does, therefore, becomes a marketing plan on how to get people to buy into this whole faith thing. How do we make Jesus more attractive/cool/accessible/entertaining/relevant? Instead of looking at Jesus as the Savior who has come for sinners, we approach evangelism and discipleship as if we were marketers.

How then do we stop selling Jesus and start engaging Millennials with who He is? Relationships.

> How then do we stop selling Jesus and start engaging Millennials with who He is? Relationships.

INTENTION, NOT AGENDA

It was a pastors conference. The main speaker—a Boomer—was doing a great job talking about how to connect with Millennials. He had some great points.

"Millennials want authenticity! You can speak to hard topics around Millennials! Be open to relationships!" This was all good stuff. I hoped the other pastors at my table would hear it. The speaker then had us turn in together at our table to talk about how we saw these things play out in our churches.

First, several of the pastors looked to the guy sitting next to me and asked, "Well, what do you think?" While this pastor was younger than them, he was solidly in Generation X, but he had been a pastor longer than I had.

Then I heard the pastor sitting next to me say, "I want to hear from Ted. He's actually a Millennial."

I took a deep breath and began: "Our church does these things naturally—"

And that was as far as I got.

Because immediately the table interrupted: "You know what young people want is relationship! They need it, and we have to be able to give it to them!"

I'd been shut down, cut off, and referred to as "they." I was going to go on and say that we have a brilliant group of people at our church. That our leadership is made up of people from all generations. But we also have key leaders who are Millennials. What the speaker had just shared is how we live. I was going to share that you need to find Millennials in your church or life, buy them a coffee, a burger, or a beer (or all three), and ask them about their experiences. But instead I was quickly cut off and cut out of any form of relationship.

I don't share that story to make you pity me. I share it because it is the narrative of the Millennial generation. We constantly feel talked at and over by those in older generations. We all have a story where we were trying to share something about our peers but were quickly shot down because we don't have enough experience. But what is not being taken into account is that our experience about Millennials doesn't come from books or speeches. It comes from living and breathing the Millennial culture. When someone talks about Taylor Swift, Beyoncé, and Kanye, we can easily carry on a conversation with them. Our communications come in the form of **gifs** and **emojis**, but we don't use them because they are faster; we use them because they are funny and sarcastic. We have lived on the front lines of this generation day in and day out for years but are constantly told we don't know what we are talking about when it comes to matters of how the Church today can connect with our generation. Our heart is for relationship, not for being told how wrong and destructive we are while simultaneously being shooed out the door because the grown-ups are talking.

What, then, does it look like to be in relationship with Millennials? I'm glad you asked.

Connecting to People without Agenda

One major thing you can do to build relationships is stop trying to build relationships. Okay. Chapter done.

Are you still here? All right, I'll explain.

Relationships that start with an end goal in mind aren't real relationships. Those fake relationships are decoys as you use another person to meet your own ambitions. Going out to meet Millennials because you want your church to grow isn't a relationship. Using a Millennial in your church to "reach other Millennials" isn't a relationship. When you are thinking, Here is what this person can do for me, that is not a relationship.

Relationship is based on a love for that person, not on the gifts, talents, or resources they can give you or your church. We encourage you to get to know Millennials because we think that when you sit down to get to know one . . . you might like one.

Here we want to mention again Paul and Becky, the self-titled "silverbacks" of our church. When Chelsey and I moved back to Texas after seminary, my call was to plant a church. Our church would not exist today without Paul and Becky. This couple walked with us the entire way. They invited us over for dinner, they talked with us passionately about not only the Church but also TV, movies, and books. They cracked jokes. We were their friends long before I was their pastor. Recently, I sat in a library next to Becky as we helped a local middle school prepare to send some books off to the school district warehouse. I was reminded once again what an incredible blessing it was to sit and laugh with her as we worked. Since the beginning of our friendship, they cared about us in real relationship.

Relationships are focused on loving your neighbor, with the reward being loving your neighbor. This is incredibly important in both our culture and in moving relationally between what always seems to be a widening generational gap. One thing you will find in connecting with Millennials is that many will hold views differing from your own. I'm not saying this in the way that when you meet different people they might hold different views than you. What I am saying is that Millennials have been bombarded with a different worldview, foundationally, than older generations have. From TV shows to books, songs to education, Millennials grew up in a culture that had shifted in significant ways from the generations before it. Some of this may show itself in good ways, such as a care for creation that mani-

Relationships are focused on loving your neighbor, with the reward being loving your neighbor.

fests itself in seeking ways to recycle and use renewable energy. At other times, this may surface as worldviews that do not connect with the views the Church has held for many years. Things like the importance of regularly being in worship or the place of church in the culture have waned over the past several years. In the last chapter, we talked about listening. This is where you get to implement those skills.

Can you listen to someone whose worldviews differ from yours? Again, I don't mean that they hold differing views on their favorite baseball team or who would win in a fight between Chuck Norris and a polar bear.[8] No, this is someone who holds views that are contrary to what you believe when it comes to faith, life, politics, and so on. The big ones. Can you hold to your beliefs without demonizing the Millennial who disagrees with you? Can you hear them without needing to correct them at every turn? As Christians, we need to be firm enough in our faith to allow people to hold contrary views. Why? Because relationships take time. Be okay with something that challenges your worldview today so that you have the voice and opportunity to challenge their worldview tomorrow.

Be okay with something that challenges your worldview today so that you have the voice and opportunity to challenge their worldview tomorrow.

This is where the fruit of the Spirit will come into play. Because, older generations, you are going to sometimes feel tempted to look at Millennials and give them what for.

MILLENNIALS, A QUICK WORD . . .

You are going to have moments where someone is talking down to you yet again and all you can think about is how quickly you will destroy their argument. Keep reading . . .

---

8   Obviously, no one would win because a polar bear would take one look at Chuck Norris and become his best friend.

But look at the fruit of the Spirit: love, joy, peace, patience, goodness, kindness, faithfulness, gentleness, and self-control. All of these things come into play in any relationship, let alone one trying to bridge the generational divide. But the work of the Holy Spirit in you will be an immense spring, welling up within you.

But Ted, what if I struggle with these things? Glad you asked. If you look at Galatians 5, Paul makes it clear that these are the fruit *of* the Spirit. They come out of you not because you have such great determination, but instead this fruit is what grows in your life when you are connected to the source. The reason the Church on earth exists is to connect people to that source: the life, death, and resurrection of Jesus. When you look at your life and see that you are struggling in the fruit of the Spirit, return to the source. Take a hard look at your life. Repent of the things for which you need to repent. Rejoice in the things in which you need to rejoice. Give thanks for the things for which you need to give thanks! Lean on the Church, be in church—that is part of her mission (Millennials, we will have a sidebar about this later). The Word of God and His gift in the Sacraments—Baptism and the Lord's Supper—will do what they are supposed to do: bring you forgiveness and renew your life. Seek them out often for this reason! Often we seek to grow in the fruit of the Spirit by sheer will. While intentionality in our faith walk is not bad, the only way we grow in these fruit is to be connected to the source. Be in the Word, be in prayer, be in the Body, be in church. Watch how God works when you run to Him. The fruit will be an outflow in your life. You will walk into conversations and relationships with this fruit because you cannot help it. The Spirit is at work within you.

Millennial Relationships

Earlier in this book, we mentioned Millennial Monday, our Monday night dinner with friends. Here is how difficult it is. At about ten on Monday morning, Lauren, one of our friends, texts us to ask what the plan is for dinner, which means we forgot to send out the text on Sunday. There is a quick discussion in our household, then dinner is decided, anything from fajitas to cereal night. A mass text is sent out, people chime in with what they can bring. People start showing up around 7 p.m.; we eat dinner, talk, play games, hang out. Around 9:30, everyone realizes they have to be up for work in the morning and starts heading home. It is incredibly simple. It's not a dinner club, book club, or any other form of club. We get together and eat, and what happens after that is usually governed by whatever we gravitate toward. But you know, we move schedules for Millennial Monday. It is a time set aside. It is our time to catch up and see how everyone is doing.

Relationships with Millennials can be incredibly simple. Not easy, but simple. And here is where I want to make sure we quickly cover something. Our Millennial Monday dinners should not become a program. Down the road, Chelsey and I don't want to hear about some church that has put together a Millennial Monday program. Here is the opportunity, Church: you can just do this. You don't need permission from your pastor, DCE, or church secretary. You just need to make time and open your home to some younger folks in your church or even just your neighborhood. Do you see some young parents who are struggling? Maybe you can set aside some time to help them out. The key is to invest in people. Here are a few other thoughts about starting a new relationship with a Millennial:

> **Relationships with Millennials can be incredibly simple. Not easy, but simple.**

DON'T BE AFRAID TO HAVE FUN!

For us, hospitality is fun. Chelsey loves to cook; I love to BBQ and grill.[9] This equals fun for us. Invite people into your home with no agenda, just a desire to form a new relationship. Watch what happens. Grab some yard games, a fire pit, or a comically large lawn chair,[xvii] and have a good time!

---

9   BBQing and grilling are two VERY separate things.

COMMIT TO BE REGULAR

In a day and age where all of our friends are starting blogs or podcasts, I can tell you that the first major factor in building up said endeavor is consistency. Blogs and podcasts that have staying power are the ones that stick to a consistent and regular posting schedule. If you are going to invest in someone, it takes time. Maybe it is weekly coffee, dinner every other week, or you meet on Tuesdays for a five-minute doughnut break between meetings. Stay consistent.

DON'T MAKE IT MANDATORY

Feel free to invite some Millennials over, even double-check to see if they are coming, but don't make it mandatory: "If you commit today, you commit forever." Let people feel free to come and go, but watch what happens with the folks who stick.

Some Quick Connectors

Are you trying to connect with that Millennial in your life but you have no idea who Lil' Sebastian is, what makes Beyoncé so great, or the purpose of Instagram? Don't feel bad. We're going to give you some quick insight into some current events and media things that might be great connectors to younger generations.

Sports—Find out what their favorite team is and why. Everyone has a story behind what team they cheer for and who their favorite player is.

YouTube—New media has been pioneered by Millennials. Some are heavily invested in it and keep up with various YouTube channels on a regular basis. Others just watch the videos that go viral. There is a Gen-X pastor friend of ours who every once in a while spends time watching popular YouTube videos and getting caught up. He calls this cultural exegesis. He says it teaches him about the culture going on around him. Here are some YouTube channels you might be interested in:

• Good Mythical Morning

• The Late Late Show with James Corden

• The Tonight Show with Jimmy Fallon

• Schmoyoho (famous for their Autotune the News clips)

TV Shows—Millennials consume all kinds of TV. For better or (mainly) worse, it is for our generation that the term *binge watching* was coined. We are experts in watching an entire season or even a series in a day or two. Not proud of it. Just stating the facts. Our recommendations for shows to connect you to the Millennial ethos are *The Office* and *Parks and Recreation*.[10] These two shows are ones most often seen and quoted by Millennials.

The Arts—Millennials love art. They love music. Ask them what they are into, what band is on their current playlist. There are some great resources out there for music now, from Pandora to Spotify; you have access to check out the music "the kids" are listening to without having to ever pay for it!

These are just some ideas. They are not the be-all, end-all to connecting with Millennials. In fact, you may start watching *Parks and Recreation* and find you hate it. That's okay! You have no soul,[11] but it's really okay. What we are saying is this: what do you connect with when you find friends in your own generation? It is likely there are Millennials out there with the same interests.

---

10   It is our recommendation to Wikipedia the synopses of seasons 1 and 2, while truly starting to watch in season 3.
11   You do have a soul. This is just a joke.

MILLENNIALS, TAKE A KNEE. LET'S HAVE A CHAT.

We just gave ourselves a ton of credit. We told our friends in older generations about relationships, our desire for them, and how we love them. We think we are pretty good at them. Now here's the deal: you, we, need friends of older generations. Those relationships are key to our growth not only as human beings but especially in the faith. While we are trying to make sure people in other generations have a ground-level view of what is going on in our generation, we need to step up to the plate as well.

First of all, invest! Our tendency is to be incredibly **ADD**. We find something new, and we run off and do it. In talking with older generations in church leadership, this is one of the frustrating things they mention: our inability to commit to something. As a Millennial leader in the Church, I am frustrated by this too! It seems the new normal of going to church is to show up once a month. Stop it. You are never going to build relationships if you only show up every once in a while. Invest where you are. Find a local church. Commit to being there a majority of the time over three months. Watch what God does! Traveling the world is an incredible thing, seeing new things is an incredible experience. Want to know what else deepens your growth as a human? Investing in your local community.

Invest in relationships with people who are in generations older than you and learn to listen. Come in with the best questions you can think of and listen, really listen, to the wisdom these people have accrued. When you commit to a lunch, coffee, doughnut, or whatever, be there, and be on time. (If you are running late, send a text letting those people know you are a little behind.) You've got it in you! There are so many great people out there in the older generations who want to invest in you. They are incredibly excited that you are still in the Church. Let them know how that excites you!

PROGRAMS

Now we're here. To the P-word . . . *Programs.* Yikes. Programs are not bad things. But all too often, programs, a structured form of ministry movement, can become about the program instead of about the people it was meant to reach.

Here are a couple of things some Millennial pastors have told me:

I think Millennials value relationship over program more so than previous generations. . . . I would say that most of them (if not all) are here [in the Church] because of connections with other people. I would say this is a contrast from my Gen-X members and Boomers who . . . are here because of the programs. There are two important things with this:

1. *If you want your Millennial pastor to leave, push him into running a lot of programs where he cannot find a relational value.*

2. *Don't expect that just because you get a Millennial pastor, he is going to fix your Millennial problem.*

Millennials need to connect with people, and they are not all going to connect with your pastor. The Church must be the connection point. Many of my Millennials have connected with Boomers.

How about we start with this: programs are not bad. There are incredibly powerful programs that have helped shape and form the lives of many people. Recovery programs, confirmation, Bible studies, small groups, all of these are great and valuable things! However, when your programs become the end in and of themselves instead of relationship being the goal, you have lost sight of what is important.

Certain programs continue the mentality that Millennials are part of a prolonged youth group. Every time a presenter, pastor, or church leader proposes reaching Millennials by some program, we Millennial pastors cringe. Again, it's not that programs are bad, but they are not going to be the silver bullet you are looking for to connect with Millennials, let alone bring them back into the Church. Let's all agree on this: silver bullets are great for two things—the Lone Ranger's guns and killing werewolves. If your response to a declining Millennial demographic in your church is to try to build a bigger, better program to entice them back, you are fighting an uphill battle.

Here is another piece of wisdom from another Millennial pastor:

> The programs . . . are all great and fun, but if they are not directly leading to people coming to know who the Christ is or coming to a deeper knowledge of Him, then they are wasted time. The Country Club mentality is gone. I don't want people to come to my church because it gives them better connections for work, for school. . . . I want people to enter our doors and to come back because this is where they learn about Jesus.

With all that being said, there are programs that work with Millennials—those that offer opportunity to build relationships. A sister church plant in our area runs a program called Pub-ology. Once a month, people from the church get together over a pint at a local brew pub and have a speaker discuss a hard topic. They have covered ideas ranging from the importance of ethics to the foundations of truth. There is then time afforded for questions and answers along with discussion with your friends. The Millennial draw for this is incredible. Why? The speakers are tackling hard topics in an open and honest way while allowing room for discussion. Their goal is not that "Pub-ology" becomes the biggest and best program but that people would come and discuss hard issues together. Do you know what that leads to? Relationships.

Another type of program that can be beneficial for connecting with Millennials? Programs that seek to serve. What are some ways you can serve the less fortunate in your community? Are you doing anything to combat sex slavery? Is there a local school that needs help with tutors? Building programs around service and inviting Millennials to join you in serving is an incredible way to build relationship through programs. Not only are you serving and targeting an itch the Millennials like to scratch, but service projects often give time set aside for conversation to happen. Often people are more willing to come serve with you before coming to church with you. Programs that promote service help people connect.

There is a craze right now in churches all across America to find the perfect program that will bring Millennials back into the Church. The truth is there's not a perfect program. Stop trying to bring Millennials back in with the best program you have. Instead, be the Body of Christ in your daily lives.

It might mean pulling back on program time for more relational time. Let me address this directly to people on church staffs across the nation: are you readily making time each week for relationships? And I don't mean that meeting you have to have for VBS. I mean simple time to catch up with people from church? This is a key way to connect with Millennials. Make it part of your workweek. Pastors, allow this time for your staff. It might mean pulling back on some programming, but it will be well worth it in the long run. In our one and a half years of existence as a church plant, I can say without a doubt that this has taken place, especially in connection to our college-age kids. They will come to a small-group Bible study I run and that time is worthwhile! But more often, it is in one-on-one coffees and lunches where I get to hear the hearts of these kids, what they are struggling with and what they are finding joy in, where I see some incredible growth in their faith.

RECLAIMING A HEALTHY VIEW OF VOCATION

One amazing piece of the Lutheran heritage is the idea of vocation. This, simply stated, is that whatever you are doing, do it in obedience to God and for His glory. It is a freeing idea that allows you to seek to follow God where He has already placed you instead of constantly waiting at the starting line for the "Big Thing" God is calling you to do.

Are you a parent? Be the best parent you can be, obeying God and for His glory.

Are you a neighbor? Be the best neighbor you can be, obeying God and for His glory.

Are you an astronaut? If you are an astronaut reading this book, I would like to buy you coffee and discuss all kinds of things, but also, be the best astronaut you can be, obeying God and for His glory.

Our mistake is to think that in reaching out to another generation we have to do some specific thing and follow some specific script in order to be effective. If you want a script, here it is again:

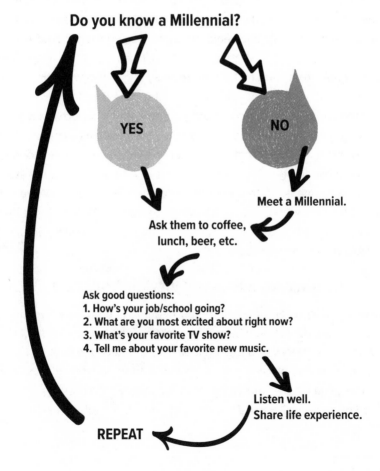

Do you know a Millennial?

YES

NO

Meet a Millennial.

Ask them to coffee, lunch, beer, etc.

Ask good questions:
1. How's your job/school going?
2. What are you most excited about right now?
3. What's your favorite TV show?
4. Tell me about your favorite new music.

Listen well.
Share life experience.

REPEAT

We often think that what we need to do is go someplace grand to serve God. But what if you started in your grocery store? Or with the buddy you drive to work with every day? Or in your home? Love people where God has placed you! Now this doesn't mean that God won't call you into more or different vocations; it is His prerogative to do that, but you are free to serve and love people where you are!

Vocation lifts from us the burden of having to do evangelism all ourselves. When we live out our vocations, we can find that it is simpler to meet people who don't know Jesus where they are. So often we get caught up in where we have to go that we forget where Jesus has already placed us. Maybe getting to meet someone and build relationships happens in the front yard as our kids are playing, in the meeting room before or after our weekly staff check-in, or while we wait in line for our coffee. The point is not that we are to constantly seek over-the-top places to go and meet people in order to share Jesus with others, but instead to open our eyes to the people He already has put around us. What vocation doesn't excuse is not getting to know our neighbors. In fact, when rightly understood and lived out, getting to know our neighbors is a key point of vocation! We cannot simply check out because we have so tightly boxed ourselves in to our idea of vocation(s) that we never connect with the strangers around us. Instead, remain open to where the Holy Spirit is guiding us.

> **So often we get caught up in where we have to go that we forget where Jesus has already placed us.**

Let me tell you about a theory Chelsey and I have developed while in the throes of church planting. We have dubbed it the "Grandmother Theorem." This theorem states that if you have a chance to present in front of grandmothers, you take it. Want to know why? In our country today, there is no one, as a whole group, praying more wholeheartedly that their grandchildren, nieces, nephews, and really any relation under the age of 32 would know and seek to follow Jesus than grandmothers. Time and again we hear the phrase, "My grandma heard you speak and told me I should come check out your church." Grandmas lean into their vocation! They have years of relational investment built up with their grandkids, they are constantly praying that they would follow Jesus, and when the time comes, they encourage them to join a church. If only we all could be a little more like our grandmas!

But here's the truth. We can be. It is really that simple. Again, simple. Not always easy. Time is the key ingredient. Pay attention for an opportunity to share the hope of Jesus. To connect Millennials to a church, you don't have to go out on the corner and set up a program that gives away free beer and doughnuts to Millennials (although it might be a big hit). You just need to be present in your vocations and pay attention to how you can glorify God in those positions.

SIMPLE BUT HARD

If you are to get a tattoo commemorating your reading of this book, it should read thusly: Simple but Hard. We give you full permission to make it as artsy or as simple as you want. But this is a phrase that should stick in your mind.

Relationships are simple but hard. They take time, a big investment of your time, your talent, and your treasure. Expect it to take more time than you wish. Think weeks instead of days, years instead of months. But keep plugging away. Recently, a wise pastor asked me how church planting was going. My response was that it is challenging but going well. His wisdom? He said, "Isn't it amazing what we think we can do in the short term and what God can do in the long term?"

That is the attitude you need going into relationships with Millennials. Don't think of the short term. Think of the long term. Where is God taking this relationship in a year, in five years? Put in the hard work. Yes, the work is hard, but it can be so simple. Invite Millennials you know out for a coffee, lunch, or a beer. Invite them over for dinner and ask them if they need any tips for home ownership—or financial planning. Offer to let them borrow your tools in case they don't have the right one for the job.

Teach them how to make your award-winning apple pie or how to smoke the perfect brisket. Ask them to show you their favorite restaurant, ask them about their music and TV shows. Invest. Simple but hard.

Relationship isn't only about generation to generation. Drew and Andrew, the guys we talked about from the brewery earlier? They want to start a Bible study. In the brewery. Because they want to grow in their faith around other men of God. They want to tackle life together in the faith. All because we have breakfast tacos once a week and hang out at the brewery. This isn't a localized event, either. People, men and women, are looking and seeking these kinds of relationships, and these relationships are an especially important key to connecting with Millennials. Really, relationships are an important key to connecting with anyone. But don't do it because there is something you can gain from it. Instead, seek to live in relationships where you are connecting without sneaky motives. You are truly seeking simply to love your neighbor.

Don't forget that every Millennial is not the same. We as Millennials will seek to remember that not all people in the older generations are the same. Instead, walk into relationships looking for the good in people. Allow Millennials to say stupid things. Because it will happen. We will. But please also have a heart that hears things from our angle, hear how deeply we have struggled with being painted with such a broad brush.

Programs aren't having the same impact with Millennials as they did with older generations. Instead of mourning this fact, look at how things you do as a church could pivot to include a more relational bent. Don't trash your programs or Bible studies. They still do a lot of good! Just seek ways that you can allow for relational time. It might mean hanging back and intentionally touching base with Millennials or asking them to grab a coffee afterward. But seek to build that connection.

Invest in relationship, and watch what God does.

DISCUSSION QUESTIONS

1. What are some good relationships you have been in? What were the attributes of these friendships?

2. What are some ways you can invest in relationships with Millennials? Millennials, how can you invest in relationships with older generations?

3. What are some of your vocations? What kind of relationships are around them?

4. What's your favorite TV show? Why?

5. Take some time and pray that God would reveal some people across generations whom He is placing in your way for the sake of relationship.

DO IT

Meet somebody new. Bonus points if they are from a different generation.

COMMUNITY

Chelsey

M illennials highly value community. We value it so much, in fact, that it drastically affects every single sphere of our lives, from the places we live and the ways we work to the entertainment we consume. One of the most accurate ways the values of popular culture can be studied is through television and its changes throughout the decades. Over time you can see the different values of community as they are explained through television. A prime example of this is the changes seen in the children's show *Scooby Doo*.

GENERATIONAL DIFFERENCES IN TELEVISION

When *Scooby Doo* first began in 1969, it was a cartoon with a highly rational and modern method of investigation (*Look! The monster was just old Mr. Jones wearing a mask the whole time!*). All the mysteries had a rational explanation; nothing was left without a solid answer. In later iterations, however, *Scooby Doo*'s characters were faced with impossible conclusions (*Look! Old Mr. Jones was really just a monster wearing a mask the whole time!*). This shift is a clear indicator of our culture's shift from modern to postmodern thought; that is, we as an American culture were not willing to accept ambiguity in the sixties, but we became more so as time went on.

I think there are other conclusions that can be drawn from popular television shows. Different generations value different things when it comes to community, and we can observe a few hit shows to find evidence of these differing values.

For instance, when the show *Cheers* was first broadcast, the inherent communal aspect was that of a "third place," or, a place "where everyone knows your name." In fact, *Cheers* was so dependent upon the third place that no action outside the bar was shown until the first episode of the second season.

Written for a Baby Boomer audience (with eleven seasons running from 1982 to 1993), the show was about a community of adults who were trying to figure out societal themes like social class, addiction, and other issues that Boomers struggled with when they began in the workforce. The characters' sense of satisfaction was not necessarily connected to their jobs—rather, they worked their jobs so that they could spend time away from them, at the third place (the bar).

"First places" are considered one's home, as well as the people who live within it. The "second place" is the workplace—where people may actually spend most of their time. "Third places" are defined as anchors of community life and foster broader, more creative interaction. The following criteria may help to accurately distinguish a third place: it's free or inexpensive, highly accessible (within walking distance for many who congregate there), has regulars, and is perceived as welcoming and comfortable.

Now, third places are still very much popular by today's standards. This description might cause you to think about a barbershop or a café or a bar, just like *Cheers*. It might even make you think of your local church—and good for your church if it does! Third places are wonderful, and they're instrumental in bringing people together; I would just like to hypothesize that the generations who depend on them for community are older ones. The third place of the bar in *Cheers* is what made the show work; after all, without the bar, there was no show. Certainly Millennials also value and frequent third places, but their sense of community is not dependent upon them. In fact, many Millennial communities have no physical space, as we'll explore later in this chapter.

Next, let's take a look at *Friends*, which first aired in 1994 and aired for ten seasons, ending in 2004. This show also had an element of the third place (Central Perk), but the plot was not constructed around this space. Instead, the plot was about six friends in their twenties, trying to figure out what to do with their lives, very much connected to their careers or lack thereof. This was a key difference from *Cheers*, which makes sense, since *Friends* was generally geared toward a Generation X audience that included some of the very first Millennials. The action took place in several different venues, and the characters tended to live together off and on in the same building—or in locations nearby. This was much more of a "you make your own family" kind of theme, which was relatable to the grown-up "latchkey children" of the eighties, who often report feeling abandoned or lost between the mammoth generation before them (Baby Boomers) and the mammoth one after (Millennials).

Next, let's take a look at *How I Met Your Mother*, which is very similar to *Friends*. *How I Met Your Mother* began in 2005 and was framed as an adult character telling his children the story of how he met and fell in love with their mother, his wife. While *How I Met Your Mother* seems nearly identical to *Friends*, there is at least one major key difference: the group of friends is actually a family of choice.

The *How I Met Your Mother* characters behave and meet together much like the characters of *Friends*—they have a third place, a bar called McLaren's—and they also move in with one another or live nearby. They struggle to find satisfaction in their careers and in their love lives, but the theme of the show is much more familial than that of *Friends*. The arc of the show is about a "family" of friends, but also about a real flesh-and-blood family and how they came to be.

The popularity of this show demonstrates a shift in the importance placed upon familial relationships by Millennials. This importance of such relationships can be observed more fully in the show *Modern Family*, which began airing in 2009. The show is about the patriarch of a large extended family of people and their daily misadventures. It certainly includes elements of the other popular shows named before, but the center of the show has always been the familial community.

This Millennial shift toward putting more importance on familial relationships can also be seen in recent popular shows like *Gilmore Girls*, *Parenthood*, and *This Is Us*, all of which deal with complicated family communities.

Of course, there have been very popular shows written by and enjoyed by Millennials that are not family oriented and that function much more like *Cheers*, including *The Office* and *Parks and Recreation*. These are both about "second places," or workplaces and the relationships fostered there. And obviously, there have been television programs in earlier decades that have followed familial relationships (such as *All in the Family*, *Family Matters*, and *The Fresh Prince of Bel-Air*), but there is no denying that the Millennial generation seeks meaning in their familial relationships and relationships with elder generations—and they like to see this behavior reflected and explored within their chosen entertainment. If they didn't, new shows about families wouldn't be doing so well.

To put this another way, I am very certain that you picked up this book expecting to see at least one mention of those pesky Millennial adult children who won't grow up, get a job, and move out of their parents' basement. While the reasons causing this phenomenon are explored more fully elsewhere in this book (a recessive economy, higher costs of living, and a general sense that one's work ought to reflect one's values other than just providing financial security), I think some reasons why this is are worth exploring here.

COMING HOME

I won't lie about this: I desperately wanted to move home after living away for four years. Well, I didn't want to move into my parents' house, but I definitely wanted to be near them.

This is not uncommon, either. Of course, there are always exceptions to the rule, but many of my friends wanted to be near their parents and extended families when they decided to settle down.

Millennials, unlike many before them, are not necessarily seeking to "get out" of the places where they grew up. They normally move away at first, of course, to attend college or other adult pursuits, but most actually move home because they value their familial communities.

"I just love the feeling of all of my extended family packed into one house," said my sister-in-law to me last Christmas. "It makes me feel very grown-up—us crammed into guest rooms, tripping over one another, sharing meals, taking walks."

Contrary to popular stereotypes, Millennials actually do care what older generations think. They value your opinions, your experience, and your time. They crave your mentorship. They want to build tight-knit familial communities, and they most likely want to include their parents, siblings, grandparents, and extended family members. Where this is not possible or healthy, many will find other extended families with which to connect. The Church has an opportunity to be the community, the extended family, that so many Millennials are seeking.

How Can the Church Capitalize on This?

One of the most brilliant ministries I ever witnessed was that of a university chapel that encouraged those in its older generations to "adopt" a college student by having them over for dinner at least once a month. This was so important to the college students—not only were they receiving a home-cooked meal instead of dorm cafeteria food, but a real family was welcoming them into a real home. These were not perfect families, either. They had messy houses, misbehaving toddlers, and sometimes dinner was Hamburger Helper. But these families took the students in, and it was one of that community's most popular ministries.

Maybe this is something your church could easily do. Or perhaps it's even simpler; perhaps you are willing to mentor a college student, young professional, Millennial mom, or even a whole family in the congregation. Notice that this is a program, but it is a program with a clear relational mission. In chapter 8, Ted talks more about what it means to be a mentor, but setting up such a process in your church fosters the growth of community. This would be especially invaluable if the Millennial does not have an existing familial relationship in the area.

And of course, the most obvious answer to this Millennial phenomenon would be to make your church itself feel like an extended family. Think on this: in your church, how many extended families do you have? I don't necessarily mean extended families of blood relation, but instead think of it as a population size. Let's put a number on that. For argument's sake, let's say a low number would be twenty and a high number fifty. In your church, how many extended families do you have? Right now our church is small but growing, so we have enough people for about one extended family, right around fifty. When we get together for community, it feels like a family reunion. Our family includes everyone from infants to retirees. Sometimes we break this into smaller groups for Bible studies or events specific to youth.

Churches would do well to connect Millennials to communities within their congregations that mimic a family reunion: old people, young people, married people, single people, babies, and more, who meet together to eat and serve and study the Bible, but who also gather with the church at large every week for worship.

MILLENNIALS, LET US REASON TOGETHER . . .

Remember when we told you earlier that you didn't need permission? You still don't need permission. If you are seeking out community, start community. It doesn't matter whether you are married or not; have kids or not, you, too, can start community. Just start inviting people over. Keri, whom we talk more about in the book, has started creating community around mud. Yep, mud. She found her kids loved to play in it. Now she invites other moms over to let their kids play in the mud. They run a hose in the backyard to make some mud, the kids play, and the parents hang out together. The last Facebook post concerning this also stated there would be massages available, from a masseuse, for those who wanted to pay for one. Building community is something that is in our generation's DNA. Capitalize on it!

Here are a couple of examples of some things we do at our church to bring our community together:

» Ted and Friends' ____ Annual Super Bowl Party (fill in the blank with the year; this was the third)—There are varying stories about how this party started. Some say Ted invited himself over and asked for a party to be thrown. He would say he simply asked to watch the game with friends. Now in its third year, it's a blast. It is truly a family reunion. People bring food, kids are running and playing, and it all happens at a house that sits on some land. The amazing thing? Our church's college kids drive thirty minutes to join us. It is everyone together.

» Summer Nights at the Brewery—During the summer, our church intentionally rests from the business of the rest of the year. But we do have monthly time together. We head up to Rentsch Brewery and rent the place out, inviting anyone who wants to come. It is a great night of games, good beer, soda for those not having beer, and catching up with people throughout the summer.

» Christmas Party—This is simple. We ask everyone to bring "Your Famous" with them. Your famous Christmas cookies, candy, dish, cheese ball. Really, the sky is the limit. It is a time for us to be together as a family before the craziness of the holidays sends us all in different directions.

» Sunday Mornings—Worship is a great thing to experience as a family. We have even had a family grow from just the grandparents to three generations in church together on Sundays! It is important to be intentional around your worship service. Once worship gets started, that is our main focus, which builds community in itself. But before church gets rolling, we have a pour-over coffee bar. We know it's the most hipster thing ever, but we did it with intentionality. Instead of running by and simply grabbing your cup of coffee, someone serves it to you. Sometimes you are waiting for the next pot to be done. But it facilitates community because there is always a chance for connection. Kids are encouraged to attend worship too. We love hearing toddlers' incoherent ramblings!

Between these big events, we work to be in the Word together. These groups are often a little more age-specific for college students, kids, parents, young adults, and so on, but they function to keep our community connected to the life-giving nature of the Scriptures.

Creating community is simple. You just need to show up somewhere and hang out. Now, what you have to understand is that creating community is structurally organic. "Organic" gets thrown around so often to be synonymous with carefree, spontaneous, or worse, unplanned. But we would argue that every organism has a structure. If you are throwing a party for community time, it is pretty simple. You will need food, people, and a place to party. Don't make it complicated. Set up structures around your community that push responsibility out to members of that community. Over the years, Ted and I have discovered that the organic-ness will show up when people spend time together. This has been present in everything from dinners with friends to planting a church.

It is important for community to include all generations. There will be times when you need to be with people in your walk of life, but the family reunion–style of community is an incredible blessing to all those who are a part of it.

CLOSED-AIR DORMS, SHARED LIVING SPACES, AND TINY HOMES

Our alma mater, Concordia University Texas (CTX), pulled off a historic move in 2008.

The university began in 1926 as a boarding high school for young men who wanted to become church professionals, like pastors or teachers. In 1926, the school was on the utmost outskirts of Austin—the main building was placed in the middle of a large pasture and only a nearby gravel path served as the road. Grandpa Doering used to tell stories of picking pecans from the groves that grew for acres around the grounds.

By 2008, however, CTX had been swallowed by the city and was bursting at the seams. In fact, our freshman dormitory was built so close to Interstate 35 that I could sit at my desk in the afternoons, look out the window, and wave to people who were stuck sitting in traffic.

CTX needed more room, so they sold the original 19 acres and moved the school to a spacious and gorgeous 389-acre campus in northwest Austin. The new campus had been home to a think tank for an oil company, so many of the buildings were already there, but some, like the dormitory, had to be built.

The dorms were new and nice, but they had an unintended effect on community life on campus: they stifled it. The residence halls were not halls. They had open-air walkways, like you see in apartment complexes.

Dorms on the old campus had closed-air hallways. You would walk down the hallway, stopping in to see your friends as you walked because if anyone was in their room, they would leave their door open. In Texas, the extreme heat and animal populations (especially on a campus next to a nature preserve, as CTX is) make it impossible to leave an exterior door propped open. Thus, the open-air hallways cut students off from one another in a way they had not been before.

Now, this was not done intentionally, of course, and CTX has done marvelous things in the past eight years to build community back up. There were great studies and reasons to have open-air hallways, but no one thought about what it might do to community. I am a proud alumnus and always will be. But I do hope (and have spoken about this to many people at the university) that the next residence hall will be built in such a way as to foster community.

Living in community is not particular to the college experience, either. We know many Millennials who have chosen to live with roommates even after graduating from college. There are two major financial reasons: the cost of living continues to rise in certain parts of the country and the cost of rent follows that same rise (sometimes at a steeper rate). In places like Austin, San Francisco, and New York, it is not surprising to find groups of people living together into their late twenties and early thirties because the cost of rent continues its upward march.

Currently, one of HGTV's most popular program themes is tiny living. This lifestyle is explored in shows like *Tiny House Hunters* and *Tiny House, Big Living*. Millennials seek lower-cost methods of living, some even going so far as to build their own tiny homes.

A college student at the University of Texas decided to build his own tiny house on wheels. It cost him about $20,000 to build, and as a result, he managed to graduate debt-free. This price, coupled with the tiny home's ability to be parked wherever the owner has permission, and thus, the ability to travel, is highly attractive to Millennials.

We personally know two couples who live in travel trailers. Our friends Tim and Sarah restored an old Airstream trailer and now live in it full time. Tim, like many Millennials, works remotely. He is a talented graphic artist, and he rents a room as an office from a friend so that he has space to work during the day.

Two Millennial alumni from CTX, Heath and Alyssa, are another good example of a mobile couple. Right after they were married, they decided they wanted to quit their "desk jobs" and go on an adventure. They bought an old RV and made a goal to visit every state in the country in it. While they were in each state, Heath worked for one day in an hourly job while Alyssa filmed the experience. They made this footage into a documentary called *Hourly America*. They have since been featured on Fox, CNN, CBS, and many blogs and websites. These days, they maintain a blog and a podcast, and they have written a book. They give advice on how to travel cheaply and have spoken at length about how they use living in their RV to their benefit by visiting all sorts of beautiful places in North America. And they do all this while they work and pay off their college debts. (If you're interested, you can read more about them here: www.heathandalyssa.com.)

In each of these stories, there are a few common threads. First, all of these people value education, but they also value financial independence, and they're willing to take radically different measures in order to achieve these goals. Second, they cannot own a bunch of "stuff" while they live this way, so they are frugal with their money and their space. They, like many Millennials, probably buy few but high-quality items. Third, while these people may seem to be cut off from their communities and families due to the transient nature of their small and mobile living spaces, they aren't. They maintain these communities online and by being able to pick up and move easily back to wherever their communities might be whenever they feel like it. With the ease of travel and the ability to work remotely also comes the ease of visiting faraway family members and friends.

For good or ill, adventure has become a key component of the Millennial psyche. To achieve this, they are cutting back on "normal," "American dream" kinds of things. Cars and houses have taken a hit[xviii] as Millennials take longer to settle down in an effort to live in more urban environments and go to see as much of the world as they can.

But what about community when you are traveling all over the place? While face-to-face familial community is important to Millennials, there is also something to be said for this generation's ability to create and maintain these relationships even from great distances. The Internet is absolutely instrumental and crucial in this respect.

HELPING THEIR COMMUNITIES

The rise of businesses like TOMS Shoes and Warby Parker have become extremely successful because they want to help communities around the world. These two companies formed the foundation for a new type of business model: social enterprise. With TOMS, for every pair of shoes you purchase, a pair is sent to someone who needs shoes. Warby Parker does the same thing, but with eyeglasses. These were Millennial businesses: those that cared for the world while seeking to make a profit.

Social enterprise is a real concern for this generation. Nearly everything Millennials buy is under scrutiny, including food. We have many friends who will buy only certain types of coffee or chocolate because they know the story of the company, know they are giving fair wages and prices to the farmers who grow these products.

The concern about food can go even further: Millennials want to eat organic, local food. We love to eat at farm-to-table restaurants and are generally incensed at the things the FDA allows in American food, particularly when so many GMOs and additives are outlawed elsewhere in the world. Not only are we concerned about health, but we also want to help the "little guys"—our friends and community members who are doing their best to fight the big companies of the world as they raise ethical food or produce handmade, artisanal goods. We want our communities to be healthy and unique, and we spend our money accordingly.

Additionally, we want our local ecosystems to be healthy. Millennials are generally horrified at the damage being done to the earth, and we prove it with the ways we commute (carpooling, public transport, cycling, working remotely, and by purchasing cars that use less fossil fuels). We are very concerned about the state of the planet. We want to leave things better than we found them, and we want to leave them green and healthy for our children and grandchildren.

For Christian Millennials, this goes far beyond just wanting to care for the earth; it's about caring for God's creation, being active in stewardship of what God has put under our dominion. Recycling is no longer seen as an exceptional thing; it is instead the norm. Composting, gardening, canning, and buying groceries package-free are all hot-button topics within Millennial communities. Buying items that were made with a low carbon footprint is also important, as is reusing and thrifting things rather than just dumping them.

Finally, Millennials like to give back to their communities by listening to, learning about, and serving others. With familial communities comes greater generational diversity and, often, greater racial and cultural diversity. Taking the time to serve others is one of the key ways Millennials like to connect with and care for their communities.

There are several easy ways churches could incorporate these communal values into their ministries.

A local church in my area recently used their money to build a space for their worship services on Sunday morning, but they built it to also be a free child-care center for teenage high school mothers during the week. They have been able to help eight young women (and plan to help many more!) choose life for their babies in this way by offering free, high-quality care for their infants. The young women are able to finish high school and pursue further education, and some have even joined the church. A majority-Millennial staff runs this church plant, and a Millennial is the day-care director.

MILLENNIALS, LEAD THE WAY . . .

Start serving your community. Invite others into it. There is an incredible opportunity for us to step out in these ways, to be an influence for our church before they ask. Love your neighbors well, no matter where you live. Serve them. Help them. You've got this. Lead the way by doing. You don't need a seven-step plan, just do it!

Is there something your church is uniquely suited to do to help others in your community?

For instance, could you plant a community garden and create a roster of volunteers to teach local children about where their food comes from?

Could you set up a soup kitchen for those in need?

Could you offer showers, haircuts, and job training for the homeless?

Could you set up a roster of volunteers to visit or foster stray animals in rescue shelters, or visit the elderly who receive no visitors in nursing homes?

Do some of your members like to knit or crochet? Maybe they could hand out supplies to create baby hats or socks for people to use in their spare time, and then donate them to a local labor and delivery ward at a hospital. Most churches already have forms of service in their local context. Millennials are concerned about their communities, and they will want to help. If you were to pair this volunteerism with a midsize, familial community within your congregation, Millennials will be even more excited to connect.

A Sense of Community

Community comes up, time and again, in our conversations with Millennials concerning the Church. Sometimes, community can feel like that elusive beast, always right at your fingertips and always slipping away.

Here is the best piece of advice we can give you: seek community as the Church and you will build community in your church. The Church is the body of believers, all those who believe in Jesus as their Savior. Your local church is a visible piece of that blessed whole. Our encouragement would be to seek community as the body of believers. Build up the community around you; look to live in connection with your neighbors and friends. Go out as the Church, the Body of Christ, into your cities, towns, and neighborhoods. Get to know some people. What you learn about community in your neighborhood helps you to build community within your church. Stop trying to force community. Once, a church we were connected to had a speaker who emphasized the importance of having fun together. From that point on, the staff had mandatory fun once a month. So build structures (we aren't talking physical buildings here, but structures in terms of systems and guides) and allow community to happen. Community has always been a part of the Church. Church and community is pulled right out of Scripture:

> And they devoted themselves to the apostles' teaching and the fellowship, to the breaking of bread and the prayers. And awe came upon every soul, and many wonders and signs were being done through the apostles. And all who believed were together and had all things in common. And they were selling their possessions and belongings and distributing the proceeds to all, as any had need. And day by day, attending the temple together and breaking bread in their homes, they received their food with glad and generous hearts, praising God and having favor with all the people. And the Lord added to their number day by day those who were being saved. (Acts 2:42–47)

Older generations, you have been blessed to have been part of communities your entire lives. From families to churches, you know what it takes. Invite Millennials to join you. Challenge them to walk alongside you in intergenerational community. Be the patriarchs of new families, and throw a good family reunion once in awhile!

DISCUSSION QUESTIONS

1. What are some of the TV shows you watched growing up? in your early adulthood? What do you think they say about your generation?

2. Brainstorm some fun ideas for a community "family reunion."

3. What are some areas of stewardship of your community, both church and neighborhood, in which you could engage?

4. Millennials, share with the older generations what the idea of community means to you.

5. Older generations, share the same thing with your Millennials.

6. But I'm reading this book alone, so I don't have to answer that question, right? False. We are not letting you off that easy. Find Millennials or someone from the older generations and ask them what an ideal community would look like for them.

DO IT

Throw a party or host a dinner. Hang out by the pool. Just do it—connect with people. Then connect again and again.

MENTORING

Ted

Mentoring has already been discussed, but it is so important, we felt it needed its own chapter. Now, what this chapter will not be is a be-all, end-all guide on how to be a mentor. Instead, think of it as a set of tools to put in your toolbox. Being a mentor is about passing on your knowledge, expertise, example, and wisdom to the next generation. It's about walking the path with someone who is farther behind than you.

It was the summer of 2010. Chelsey and I had just gotten married in June. Obviously, the next logical step was for her to accompany me and my favorite group of high schoolers as I led a trip to the Rocky Mountains. Chelsey was a champ. Especially on our first full day at the adventure camp.

This was not a brand-new adventure for me, even though it was the first time I was in charge. When I was in youth group, we would go every other summer to a camp outside of Gunnison, Colorado. It was a week of mountain hiking, rock climbing, challenge coursing, fly-fishing, and white-water rafting. One thing stuck out in my mind from when I was in high school: the mountain hike was the hardest day. You have a bunch of young folks coming from below sea level in Houston to ten thousand feet above sea level at base camp in the Rockies. We were breathing hard just getting off the bus, let alone hiking up a mountain.

I'm athletic but not an athlete. I played lacrosse in high school and loved any game of pickup, any sport, with my friends. But climbing that mountain always took it out of me. We would start in the morning, hike up to a bowl on the mountain, and then come back down. I was always toward the end of the pack. The issue there is that there is a slinky effect. All my friends who were strong athletes would push out ahead of everyone else, but our guides from the camp would pause for a break and wait for the tail end to catch up. But the minute we caught up, the front would immediately start moving. Thus no one in the back would get a break. It was grueling—worthwhile, but grueling.

I remembered this years later when, as a leader, I had my first meeting with the camp director upon arrival. Our youth were split into three groups. Each would be doing a different activity each day. With my personality, I lean more toward the approach of a quick Band-Aid rip when it comes to things I am not fond of doing. So, as the meeting was winding to a close, we began to choose which group would do which activity when. I immediately volunteered my group for the mountain hike first. Looking back, I was pretty proud of myself for about half a second. Because that's when the hammer dropped.

"Great! We'll need your group in the mess hall at 4:30 tomorrow morning."

My eyes about popped out of my head. "Why is that?" I asked, with this new revelation that this early morning hour had not been the case when I came to this camp in high school.

"We want to summit you guys this year, which means you need to be up the mountain and back in the tree line by 11:00 to avoid afternoon thunderstorms." Dread played across my face. *Summit?* Not just partway up to a bowl, but to the top of a mountain. The Band-Aid had been ripped. But it was not the end of the pain.

The next morning we had all of the kids in our group, along with the adult leaders, in the mess hall at 4:30. We were hiking the mountain right around 5:45. To say it was a comedy of errors would be to put it lightly. We had encouraged our kids to get strong shoes, pushing hiking boots if they had them. One of our girls about forty-five minutes in had to stop because she was crying so hard she couldn't see straight. Her hiking boots were in fact steel toe work boots and about two sizes too small. We all stopped, and our guides got to work cutting out the steel toes with their pocket knives. She hiked the rest of the mountain with her toes poking out the front of her boots.

Then I noticed a strange thing. Our guides kept stopping our group and conferring. It was then that our adult leaders realized something: the guides had never summited this mountain. They had lost the trail. In their college-age wisdom, they decided that where we were going we didn't need trails. They pointed us up the mountain, and we blazed our own trail. Imagine looking up at a mountain, and instead of hiking up a switchback trail, you think, The shortest distance between two points is a straight line! That is what we did.

It was at this point that two things began to happen: I began to struggle with the altitude, and I noticed the slinky effect happening. Our group had some amazing athletes in it: kids who were varsity track stars, swimmers, and baseball players. Even coming from below sea level, they were in good-enough shape to tackle this mountain on the first day. Their pace was incredible. At our next stop, though, I pulled aside four or five of my senior leaders who fit this profile and challenged them. I looked at them and said, "I know in your mind that the challenge of this mountain is to see who can reach the top first. Who can get the victory. I want to challenge you with something else. I want you to be the ones who get this whole group to the top of the mountain." They looked at me, nodded, and that was that.

Then the most amazing thing happened. I watched a group of high school senior athletes set up a system to get their friends to the top of a mountain. One would run ahead about fifty yards to be the next goal up the mountain. The others would stay back with the stragglers, encouraging their peers that they could do it. "Listen, all you have to do is make it up to Alex. Make it to him, and we'll take a breather." When they would reach Alex, one of the seniors who hiked up with the stragglers would run ahead another fifty yards. I watched as, without a word between them as to who would do what, they leapfrogged the entire way up the side of the mountain. You know what? They got everyone up the mountain that day.

While I was being awed by the work of these teenagers, I myself was struggling to stay just ahead of them—hiking at altitude was doing a number on me. It was at this moment, as I heaved and struggled for breath, that one of our adult leaders came up to me with a simple request: "Hey, Ted, let me take your pack." Rob was an elder at the church and one of the strongest examples of a man of God I know. I didn't want to give up my pack, but all it took was a sideways glance from Chelsey, and I shrugged it off and handed it over to Rob. I didn't realize how much I needed the help he had given me. I doubt he knows how much that one sentence has changed my life.

Mentorship takes three things: investment, apprenticeship, and making room for someone else to lead. At the time, I didn't know how much hiking a mountain would show me the importance of these three things. My investment in some high school seniors gave me an opportunity to hand off leadership to them. Rob's example to me was one action in a long line of being apprenticed by believers who were in the older generation. When I thought I could handle it, that I had to carry my burden to prove my worth, Rob showed me that this is a team effort. The challenges in our lives are not meant to be lived alone; instead, we are gifted a community in which we can encounter them together.

Mentorship takes three things: investment, apprenticeship, and making room for someone else to lead.

INVESTMENT

Whom are you pouring into? Whom are you discipling? Investment is an incredible tool for mentoring. Investment is a form of stewardship—it's working wisely to build up the people placed in your life. It is also a key for connecting with the Millennial generation. Now, as we talk about investment, we will try to differentiate between investing in those in your church and those who may not know the Lord. But the principles of investment are the same. Investment takes time, talent, and treasure.

TIME

How and where you spend your time indicates what is important to you. Investing your time may be the simplest but most important form of pouring into a Millennial.

The first thing you need to know is that we are not suggesting you invest in every Millennial who walks by your office or cubicle or into your home. Exhaustion would become your new norm, and one can take only so much talk about how cool raw milk is or the importance local art.[12] But what if you started with a simple prayer: "Lord, show me a young person in whom I can invest." Start there. Then keep an eye out. Look for young people who keep running across your path, those you seem to keep bumping into. When you run into a Millennial and your conversations seem to keep going longer and longer, that's a good indication that this is someone in whom you can invest your time.

You have prayed. You have kept an eye open. The Lord has placed someone in your way. What is the next step to investment of time? It would be easy to give you a rubric specific to Millennials. To say, "Time X + Person Y = Millennial Following Jesus!" Unfortunately, that is not how it works. And our guess is that you don't have much extra time. Maybe you are running kids from practice to practice to game to choir concert. And

---

12 Please know that this is not every Millennial; we have just given you a breakdown of hipsters. Although Chelsey and I do enjoy raw milk and local art. Okay. This might be applicable to more than hipsters.

that is just Tuesday night. Maybe you are retired but incredibly active in church and your community. Carving out time would just be hard. Here is what we are encouraging you to do: don't carve out time; invite people into your schedule. You know what a mother of three young children might need? To see how a high school mom does it. That new kid on your floor at work? He might just need to see how you grind through a tough workday. Instead of looking at always carving out time, which you will need to do now and again, look for opportunities to invite a Millennial to join you and live life with you. Our guess is that you eat dinner almost every night. Possibly lunch during the day. You don't have to get fancy. Are you making spaghetti for dinner with you and the kids? Invite the Millennial to come along and bring a salad. Now that first salad might be a little small because they've only ever bought food for one, but here again is a time to invest.

> Here is what we are encouraging you to do: don't carve out time; invite people into your schedule.

MILLENNIALS, A QUICK SIDEBAR . . .

Millennials, do you look for time to spend with the older generations? It is just as important for you to invest in them as it is for them to invest in you. Are you seeking time with someone who has already walked the places you are going in your life? In this book, we are challenging older generations, quite a bit, to see things from your angle. But you also need to be challenged to see things from theirs. You can't just sit back and wait for people to approach you. Be proactive. Seek out mentors, and ask if you can spend time with them.

Time is the foundation for investment as it will be a major part of both talent and treasure.

TALENT

Where did you learn what you learned? Where did you learn to play guitar, train a dog, raise kids who love Jesus, or change a tire? The list is endless. Our guess is that you didn't start work as a young person knowing everything there was to know. You put in the time. Each day, you would put in the grind. With your family, your friends, and your career. Parenting was not an overnight success. There was that time you burned a lasagna in the oven. Your boss chewed you out because you missed a deadline. But as you grew in knowledge and wisdom, you found that you had talent. Maybe it was at work. Maybe at home. Whatever it was, you had a talent that kept growing.

How do you invest that talent? Let me give you a simple example as a Millennial. Chelsey and I bought our first home in the summer of 2016. It was an incredibly exhilarating and decidedly scary moment for us. It had taken six months and we had put in seven offers on different houses. All were not chosen, until the seventh one. As we sat in the loan office signing away our lives, I couldn't help but feel a thrill. We were homeowners! Then came the page that showed how much the house would actually cost, when you factored in interest. My heart sank into my stomach. All of a sudden, I realized just how much this would not only cost, but how much I would need to take care of it. This is where a few guys from church came into play. As the months drew on and I ran into the problems that come with homeownership, a team of older men from church became my homeowner advisers. Why? Because they had been there. They had the talent. They knew who to call to come fix a broken heater at the best price. If there was a specific tool I needed, one of them had it and would give me a tutorial on how to use it. The first time my parents came to visit, my dad's first question was, "What projects can we do?" That weekend, painting downstairs got finished and we laid a brick border around the front gardens. For the first several months, I came into church on Sunday mornings and sought out these guys to ask them questions. They had the knowledge. They had the talent.

Use your talent to mentor others. Sometimes this means an actual talent. Maybe it's cooking or baking, maybe woodworking, possibly it's budgeting. These gifts allow you to have something to share, something to give away. Your talents may be marketable skills or simply your hobby, but you have something to share.

How can you leverage those talents to help you mentor? Make time. Be available. This is that moment where we said you might need to carve out time. It might mean teaching someone one-on-one what you do. Or inviting them to come join you as you do it. We'll talk about this a little bit more when we discuss apprenticeship.

MILLENNIALS . . .

What are some areas in which you want to grow? Find someone who has that talent. Seek it out. Ask them how they do it, how they got started, and how they didn't get discouraged. Also, remember you have talent. You can share upward. I could talk about how simply being a Millennial makes you a social media expert. But I won't, because you are. How then do you share those things upward? Humbly and patiently. Realize that as you are mentored by older generations they are being, hopefully, incredibly kind and patient with you. Don't assume that just because you know something it makes you awesome. You have talents to be shared, not to puff up your ego.

TREASURE

If these investments were in a pyramid form, time would form the base because of its importance, talent would be in the middle because it is something unique that you can share, and treasure would be at the top because it is the easiest thing to do. All you have to do is have some money and spend it on a Millennial. Here is a list of some ideas:

» **Buy them food.** This is pretty self-explanatory, but it is a great way to connect. This could be as extravagant as a dinner out or as simple as a doughnut. Set up a weekly time together, grab some food, and ask them how they're doing. Find a new restaurant or food truck in town, and ask them if they want to check it out with you.

» **Buy them a beer.** At the brewery here in town, I have heard this referred to as "the beer garden life." Microbreweries are popping up all over the country. If there isn't a microbrewery, there is a bar in town. Go grab a beer or a glass of wine with a Millennial. Catch up on the week, and ask if he or she has any questions about parenting, work, or how to make your famous apple pie.

» **Get something for their kids.** Millennials are quickly becoming parents. Want to connect with those people? Get a little something for their kids. Maybe it's just something from the dollar bin at Target, but use it as an opportunity to stop by their place and love on their kids—and, by extension, them.

The sky's the limit when it comes to your treasure. But the little bit you spend on the Millennials you are mentoring shows them that they are worth it.

MILLENNIALS, BUCKLE UP . . .

You need to start investing with your treasure. We are a generation who pride ourselves on buying all kinds of clothes, coffee, and art that is sustainable, gives back to the larger community, and is fair trade. This is not bad. In fact, we should find some solace in that. But time and again, as Chelsey and I talk with leaders and pastors in the Church, we hear this line connected with our generation: "I'm glad we have Millennials, but I don't see them tithing." Now, before we get into a rant about the Church just wanting our money, please regard Jesus:

> And do not seek what you are to eat and what you are to drink, nor be worried. For all the nations of the world seek after these things, and your Father knows that you need them. Instead, seek His kingdom, and these things will be added to you. "Fear not, little flock, for it is your Father's good pleasure to give you the kingdom. Sell your possessions, and give to the needy. Provide yourselves

with moneybags that do not grow old, with a treasure in the heavens that does not fail, where no thief approaches and no moth destroys. For where your treasure is, there will your heart be also." (Luke 12:29–34)

The majority of churches are not seeking your money for financial profit. It takes money to run a church. That is a fact. But it is also an issue of our hearts and discipleship. The local church is a mission outpost of the kingdom of God. Investing in the local church (with your time, talent, and treasure) is about seeking the kingdom. Watch where you spend your money. Take some time and judge it against how you are seeking the kingdom. This is an incredible opportunity for us to take up the mantle of leadership in our churches. We start with our money, proving that the mission of the kingdom of God is something worth investing in.

APPRENTICESHIP

Mentoring should take on the form of apprenticeship. Back when everyone worked in skilled trades, you started as an apprentice. You spent years watching your master, working to learn the trade. And isn't that the way of the kingdom of God?

» Be imitators of me, as I am of Christ. (1 Corinthians 11:1)

» It was not because we do not have that right, but to give you in ourselves an example to imitate. (2 Thessalonians 3:9)

» Remember your leaders, those who spoke to you the word of God. Consider the outcome of their way of life, and imitate their faith. (Hebrews 13:7)

» Beloved, do not imitate evil but imitate good. Whoever does good is from God; whoever does evil has not seen God. (3 John 1:11)

Jesus taught His disciples by example. They followed Him around the countryside as He taught and lived. They were learning the way of their master. Apprenticeship combines both a giving of knowledge from one generation to the next along with an example to imitate. For the master, apprenticeship was not about his own glory (except in Jesus' case), but about training the next generation of masters.

While at the seminary, we had a great example of an apprenticing master. Dr. Dale Meyer, president of Concordia Seminary, St. Louis, never shied away from telling us why he was so passionate about a good seminary experience: he wanted his grandchildren to have good pastors. His goal was not the growth of his own ego, pointing to all the people he had trained in his time. Instead, his focus was on training the next generation of teachers. He invited students into his home, sat around at night discussing topics from life to doctrine, and was always available during his office hours. Dr. Meyer did his best to apprentice the student body of Concordia Seminary.

Ask yourself, "Could I take on one apprentice?"

Apprenticeship is the joy of sharing your life with another person. It doesn't have to be as intense as your job. Apprenticing is allowing someone to see your life and asking them to imitate it. The Christian's call is the same as that of Paul from 1 Corinthians: always point to Jesus. It is never simply about you; it's about pointing and saying, "Watch my example because I am following Jesus' example." What about mentoring a Millennial who might not be a follower of Jesus? You just change your approach a little bit: "Watch my example, do as I do, and let me tell you why I do what I do." Your life is an example that should point to the goodness of the Gospel no matter who you apprentice.

But what about when you fail? What about those moments where the sinner side of your saint-and-sinner dynamic begins to rear its ugly head? Be the first to repent. Let me say that again.

Be. The. First. To. Repent.

We live in a world that is always looking to pass the buck. Leadership in our culture means seeking to find someone lower than you to take the blame. As Christians, we are called to be repenters. This is authenticity in relationship. It shows that you are not perfect, but instead in need of forgiveness. Want to blow Millennials out of the water? Come to them when you mess up. Let them be present when you apologize to someone else and seek forgiveness. This is an incredible example to follow. It shows that you are not perfect—that you understand your own personal need to be forgiven. And there it is, a door to talk about the Gospel.

There is great joy to be found in apprenticeship. You are getting to share the things in this world that excite you, the passion you have found in your job, your home, or your church. It is an incredible opportunity, and you may find that while passing on something to the next generation you find out more about yourself.

We live in a world that is always looking to pass the buck. Leadership in our culture means seeking to find someone lower than you to take the blame.

An Example from Baseball Greats

Let us give you an example of master and apprentice from baseball. In the middle of the 2005 season, the Houston Astros were looking for a hitter to put them into deep playoff contention. They found that player in Carlos Beltrán. Beltrán would be a player who could hit in clutch situations throughout the end of the season and all the way to the World Series. They got to the World Series. But when they ended up losing the series, the Astros worked diligently to sign Carlos Beltrán to a long-term contract. It fell through. Every season after that, anytime Beltrán came to the plate in Minute Maid Park, he was booed by the hometown Houston crowd. They had loved him and felt betrayed when he left.

Fast-forward to December 2016. Eleven years later and a young Astros team had become contenders for the World Series title once again. Going from the bottom of baseball to playoff hopes for the second year in a row had the Astros looking for veteran talent to join the team. They signed none other than Carlos Beltrán. What was Beltrán's reason for signing with Houston? Back in 2005, the Astros had put his locker next to that of Hall of Fame second baseman Craig Biggio. Beltrán talked about how he spent the second half of the season being mentored by Biggio. Coming back to Houston, he had one request for the locker room: that they would put him next to a young kid who needed to be mentored.

When Beltrán showed up for the press announcement, two other players asked to have dinner with him, Carlos Correa and José Altuve. Correa had been Rookie of the Year two years earlier. Altuve was coming off three consecutive season ranked in the top five hitters in the American League, and in two of those seasons he had the most hits in Major League Baseball. These two young players had every right to be smug and explain to Beltrán why he needed to follow their lead in the locker room. But what did they do? After some dinner and small talk, Altuve began asking Beltrán how he could hit better. He was a young player in his prime, a top hitter in the league, but he saw a guy who was farther down the road than him, who had accomplished what he wanted to accomplish, and he asked to be apprenticed.[xix]

MILLENNIALS, SEEK A GOOD MENTOR

Seek to be apprenticed. From work to family, from personal faith to the life of the Church, find someone who is farther along in the journey than you. For us this has been a simple idea. Who is someone I want to be like? It is those people we have sought out to mentor us. When doing this, allow yourself to be teachable. Find ways to admit your weaknesses. Find someone who can teach you. When I was a kid, I so desperately wanted to learn guitar. There were two men who pushed me and allowed me to grow: John and Ray. John was my youth director who allowed me to play in the band before I was good. He worked with me and allowed me to grow. He called me out when I was not focusing and built me up after a good rehearsal. Ray was the dad of a friend. He was and is one of the best guitar players I know. He constantly encouraged us. His sons, Rylan and Reese, are now two of the best guitar players I know, and there is a group of friends who play guitar because Ray encouraged them.

MAKING ROOM IN LEADERSHIP

Millennials have been told time and again that it is not their turn, they just need to wait a little longer. But let us tell you, there are some incredible young people out there who are ready and willing to start leading. Maybe it's in church, in the school PTA, or in your company. Are you looking for the person in the next generation who will take your job when your work is finished?

At some point, we will all vacate the roles in which we work, from volunteering at church and being at home with our families to our places of employment. Time keeps marching on, and it changes our roles. Children become parents, parents become grandparents, grandparents become great-grandparents, and we all end up back in the ground. From dust we came and to dust we shall return (Genesis 3:19). Opening leadership roles to Millennials does not diminish your role—it simply allows for the next generation to take a further step in their journey.

There are three steps to the process of opening leadership to Millennials:

1. Connect them to a mentor

2. Prepare them to lead

3. Allow them to fail

Connect Them to a Mentor

Introduce a Millennial to a person who could serve as a mentor. This mentor might be you, or it might not be. Let's look at an example in the Church. A pastor or staff member cannot mentor every Millennial in your church. Nor should they. But there are different people who can. Team them up with an elder, Bible Study leader, or the head of VBS. Teach them what you know, but also let them come along to see what the job entails (time/talent + apprenticeship). Encourage leaders in your church to walk alongside the Millennials they are mentoring. Let apprentices see their mentors' tasks at church—and their lives of following Jesus outside of church too. A disciple is someone who trusts in the promises of Jesus and seeks to follow Him always.

Prepare Them to Lead

Give Millennials the tools to succeed, whatever that means in the context of where you are serving. From checklists to formal training, give the next generation of leaders what they will need to lead effectively. Then let them know that their job will be to pass on these skills to someone else, to equip the next person to lead. Have the mentor walking alongside Millennials ask what else they think they might need. Give them time in this new role, however long it seems necessary, and then release them into leadership.

Allow Them to Fail

Don't wonder whether failure will happen, just know it will. Allow Millennials to fail so you can help them pick themselves back up and learn. Be ready to share how you have failed so they do not believe they are the only ones who could possibly mess up something that you do so well. What you are doing is teaching them that failure doesn't mean they've failed as a leader; teach them that not learning from their mistakes, refusing to grow from them and moving on is what ultimately sets them up for complete failure.

Making room in leadership is passing the torch to the next generation. It may feel like you don't know anything, that you are being tossed to the side for what is new. But fight that feeling. You are moving into a new role, from chief doer to chief mentor. Handing off the reins doesn't mean letting go of things you love. It means entrusting them to the next generation because you've taught them well.

You can do this outside the Church too. Bring Millennials into leadership in these ways, and teach them what it means to grow as a leader; you'd be surprised at how much Millennials want this in their daily lives. Look for ways to encourage leadership in your places of work, your neighborhoods, and places where you volunteer. Building leadership in these ways gives you an opportunity to share things that are important to you. Church is probably one of those things. When you are able to mentor someone, you would be amazed at the things they are open to trying because they value your relationship and wisdom.

REMEMBER WHY YOU ARE DOING THIS

Why mentor? Why even try to pass knowledge on to the next generation? Because we imitate those in the faith who came before us. Scripture is full of men and women who mentored the next generation: Jethro,[13] Moses,[14] Priscilla and Aquila,[15] Lois and Eunice,[16] Paul,[17] and Jesus.[18] You are mentoring people for the sake of the Gospel.

Who is that person in your life? Maybe who are those *people*? Can you list the men and women who came before you, who nurtured your faith through mentoring? It might have been a pastor, DCE, or Sunday School teacher. Maybe it was your parents and grandparents. It could have simply been someone who took an interest in you and shared the story of Jesus. Whoever it was, this is why you mentor, for the next generation of the Church.

Mentorship is a gift of age. The only way you get farther down the road is to have traveled down it longer. This is an incredibly good gift. Being a member of the "older" generations is not at all a bad thing. When we use that term in this book, it is not derogatory. It is a declaration that

---

13   Exodus 3; 4; 18
14   Exodus 24:12–13; Numbers 27:18–23; Joshua 1:1
15   Acts 18:24–26
16   2 Timothy 1:5
17   1 and 2 Timothy
18   The Gospels

others have grown wise through the years, have the knowledge and ability to pass on what they know to the next generation.

MILLENNIALS, WE CAN DO THIS TOO!

We need to look for mentors. We need to seek out those who have gone before us so that we, too, may grow and receive what the gift of time has given to these older generations. But we must also start asking ourselves this question: How are we preparing to mentor the generations younger than us? Maybe it is younger Millennials or the next generation currently in high school. How are you investing in those younger than you? We are already an older generation; how are we seeking opportunities to invest in those younger than us?

DISCUSSION QUESTIONS

1. What are some everyday ways in which you can invest your time?

2. As you look at your life, what are some talents you think you can pass on?

3. Millennials, what are some talents you can pass upward? How are you investing your money for the next generation and for the Kingdom?

4. What are some ways you could implement apprenticeship at your church? in your workplace? in your community? across the street? Remember, don't be pushy, but take opportunities when they arise.

DO IT

Take some time to write down a list of those people who have been mentors in your faith. If you still have some way of getting in touch with them, drop them a note thanking them for their investment in your life.

EARNING YOUR VOICE

Ted

After coming this far, there is something we need to talk about: earning your voice. This is important, whether for bridging the gap between generations or just talking to your neighbor.

The Church doesn't have a problem with the truth. Over and over, we see how Scripture leads us back to truth and, in the end, it all points to THE TRUTH: Jesus. The truth is vital. But how do we communicate to others that the truth is important? There is a problem in the American church that can be summed up in the mantra "Whoever yells the loudest speaks the truth." This happens in sermons, interviews, podcasts, and on social media. Instead of people outside the Church hearing the important message we have to share about Jesus, all they hear is the hollering of yet another person trying to force their views down others' throats.

But we are told often that the world will not like what we have to say. Jesus even warns us:

> If the world hates you, know that it has hated Me before it
> hated you. If you were of the world, the world would love

you as its own; but because you are not of the world, but I chose you out of the world, therefore the world hates you. Remember the word that I said to you: "A servant is not greater than his master." If they persecuted Me, they will also persecute you. If they kept My word, they will also keep yours. (John 15:18–20)

There will be plenty of issues that no matter how hard we try, no matter how kind or gentle we can be, the world will hate us. Our message of following after Jesus is one of hope. He is our Savior. However, our message is also one of denial. Jesus tells us that if we want to be His disciples, we have to pick up our crosses daily and follow Him. In following Jesus we deny ourselves, our wants, our wishes, our desires, and our idols. The world doesn't want to hear that. They want to continue on in their ways.

What, then, are we to do? We need to live in tension. We need to earn our voices.

The "Attitude Reflects Leadership, Captain" Principle

The basics of this are simple. Ask good questions. Listen well. All of this is to earn respect. This is a major area of disconnect, especially between Baby Boomers and Millennials. In their ethos and rearing as children, Boomers were taught that respect for authority was innate in offices, positions, and elders. Gen X came along and questioned all of those things and created media around questioning authority. Millennials consumed that media. We would argue that Millennials do respect offices, positions, and their elders, to a certain degree. They respect that someone has been put in a position of authority, but that person also has the opportunity to gain their earned respect as an individual.

This can best be explained by what we will term the "Attitude Reflects Leadership, Captain" Principle. In the iconic movie *Remember the Titans*, an exchange between the characters of Julius Campbell and Gary Bertier is especially memorable. Now, if you say to yourself, "I don't think I've ever seen *Remember the Titans*," put down this book. Find a copy of *Remember the Titans*. Pop some popcorn. We'll be here when you get back.

Okay, now you've seen *Remember the Titans*. We're happy we could introduce you to it. Now, about this scene with Julius and Gary: they are in the midst of a break while running three-a-day summer football practices. Their school has been integrated and they are, at this point poorly, navigating this new reality on their football team. Gary, as the team captain, pulls Julius aside and tells him of all the wasted talent he has as he looks out only for himself instead of being a team player. Julius snaps back that until the rest of the team starts playing together, he'll look out for himself. Gary shakes his head and incredulously tells Julius that is one of the worst attitudes he's ever heard. Julius thinks for a moment, nods in self-assurance, and responds to Gary, "Attitude reflects leadership, captain."

How is your leadership affecting attitude? Do you approach Millennials as if you know their entire stories? Are you assuming they embody a particular stereotype without ever getting to know them?

If you want to impact Millennials, the reality is this: you will need to earn their respect, not just assume you have it.

MILLENNIALS, LET'S CHAT.

I know I've experienced this; I'd assume you have too. But Scripture tells us to respect our elders. I think we need to take some of our own medicine here and learn out of love for others to lean into respect instead of indignation. I have fallen into the trap of believing the worst about people simply because they rattled off some derogatory comment about "those young people." It is important for us to let respect lead the way, especially within the Church. Paul reminds us, "Love one another with brotherly affection. Outdo one another in showing honor" (Romans 12:10). Let's try to make that our motto.

A PRACTICE IN SANCTIFICATION

Earning your voice will be a hard lesson in the lifelong journey of following Jesus. The lesson is hard because it goes against our natural inclination to put ourselves first. It will mean learning to gauge your own heart, praying quick prayers for the Lord to guide your thoughts and your tongue, finding the wisdom in knowing when to speak the truth boldly, and bearing your cross. Earning your voice is about waiting and watching as the Holy Spirit works in you for the benefit of your neighbor.

Let's Be Honest

Millennials can be punks. There is no other way to put it. How can we say this for sure? We are Millennials. We have been punks. There is a high likelihood we will be again. But can you remember when you were our age? when you were young and idealistic? You were starting your first job, joining your church, and possibly starting a family. Were there points where you were a punk?

When earning your voice with Millennials, there are three things you should consider: remembering where you came from, not dismissing younger voices, and being authentic.

Remembering where you came from can be of incredible help as you connect with younger generations. There were times in your life when you were experiencing adulthood for the first time. You were growing; you were making mistakes and learning from them. There was a flood of new experiences, responsibilities, and the start of a new journey. That is where Millennials are now. We are coming into our own, discovering what the world of being an adult is like. The term **adulting** was coined to help cope with the amount of responsibility and new experiences that come with it. Instead of simply telling Millennials how good they have it because of how bad you had it, maybe try to share what it was like when you transitioned from childhood to adulthood. Help us see and understand what you struggled through. Let us learn from your wisdom.

Please don't dismiss Millennials simply because they are young. I've experienced this along with many friends of my generation. The apostle Paul encourages Timothy, "Let no one despise you for your youth" (1 Timothy 4:12). Time and again, Millennials are judged solely based on their age. They come to the table with new ideas or new ways of doing things and are simply dismissed. Story after story is told by our Millennial friends that goes something like this: " I don't even like being called a Millennial. When people realize I belong to that generation they start telling me everything that is wrong with me." No chance for dialogue. No chance for discussion. Want to blow Millennials' minds? Ask them what they think of their generation. They may not be experts in everything, but they are experts of the Millennial mind-set. They've lived it, grown up in it. The quickest way to lose your voice is to tell Millennials who they are without ever asking *them* who they are. This is a great way to connect! Millennials are open to sharing their love for and frustrations with their peers. Oftentimes, they are open to admitting the same faults you see but then will surprise you with the joys they find around them!

As we've asked Millennial after Millennial about what they look for in a church, by and large, the word thrown around the most is *authenticity*. Now, this is a buzzword. *Authenticity* has been thrown around nonstop in reference to Millennials. But what people often assume is that authenticity is connected to some new form of hipsterism. To be authentic, you need to dress like a lumberjack, have a beard to match, and work in a coffee shop. Ladies, you would need to wear high-waisted denim with a crop top and make sure you have a random streak of color in your hair. This is what authenticity must mean to Millennials. But in reality, what we want is for you to be you. Remember when we talked about how Millennials have been targeted by marketing our entire lives? We don't want you to market yourselves to us. Be you. Don't try

> As we've asked Millennial after Millennial about what they look for in a church, by and large the word thrown around the most is *authenticity*.

to impress us. Just be you. We want to get to know real people, not some sham you put up to sway people to like you. We get enough of that on Facebook. Don't give us the show, give us the substance. Earning your voice simply means that you are you, not some cooler version of you.

This will be an exercise in patience. Millennials will make you angry. They will push your buttons. They will come across as disrespectful know-it-alls.[19] But the question you have to ask is this: is it worth losing your

> **Earning your voice simply means that you are you, not some cooler version of you.**

voice, your chance to share the Gospel, to be right? There will be those moments to prove your rightness. Speaking the truth in love means that people will be offended. This will force you to work on your patience. It will mean learning to learn the hard process of knowing when to speak and when to hold back. But it is part of the process of earning your voice. And that is what we are trying to help you see as a whole—that you can connect with someone who has a different worldview than you! Jesus has a plan for reaching Millennials, and you're a part of it!

MILLENNIALS

All right. We just had the discussion of how older generations can earn their voice. Millennials. We are young. Our experience pales in comparison to the generations who have come before us. Earning our voice is also a practice in our own path of following Jesus. We are not the victims every time. We are sinners who all too often react with disrespect. We believe that anything that comes out of our mouths is a gift from on high. How could we possibly have any bad ideas? We have to stop our need for other people to fix our problems. The next time a Millennial writes a blog post about the Church and Millennials and simply points out problems while only proposing how others can fix them, Chelsey and I are going to lose our ever-loving minds. It is our job, as

---

19   A quick thank-you here to my parents and mentors who have put up with my own youthful ignorance and my superpowered ability to run my mouth.

Millennials, to seek out leaders in our lives we can listen to.

Okay. Brace yourselves. Millennials. Don't. Run. Your. Mouth.[20] Not everyone in the older generations is out to get you. They are not all against you. If all we do is talk about how the older generations ruined us and place blame on them for all of our actions, then we won't take ownership of these things for ourselves. There will be people from older generations who will attack you. No matter what you say or do, they will look down on you. But do you know how Paul finished his statement to Timothy? He said this: "But set the believers an example in speech, in conduct, in love, in faith, in purity" (1 Timothy 4:12). If Paul calls our older generations not to look down on us, the calling in our lives is to set an example in the areas stated. Running our mouths is not a way to earn our voice.

We have to stop believing that other people can fix our problems. If another story is told about how some college professor or boss has been called by a mother to ask about the performance of their child, we should take our lumps. We are not helpless. There is so much that we can do. If we want to earn our voices with generations who have come before us, let's show them that we are problem solvers, not just complainers. Look at all the good we can do. We can join churches and be strong members of our community. Let's earn our voices by showing what we can do!

Look for good leaders. Sit and listen at the feet of someone who is where you want to be someday. Earn your voice by keeping quiet, by asking good questions. This doesn't just apply to spiritual matters. There are all kinds of people from older generations out there who have knowledge they can impart to you. And when you listen, you earn your voice.

---

20   Please read this with the clap emoji between each word.

THE IMPORTANCE OF EARNING YOUR VOICE

Why subject yourself to this form of torture . . . sanctification? Because the whole point of this book is not simply for you to be besties with the Millennial next door, but rather to have an opportunity to share the Gospel. The whole point of bridging the gap, of learning about the next generation, is to pass on the faith and to do so effectively. The goal is to look for opportunities to "make a defense to anyone who asks you for a reason for the hope that is in you; yet do it with gentleness and respect" (1 Peter 3:15). Earning your voice is about having a chance to share the Gospel.

The whole point of bridging the gap, of learning about the next generation, is to pass on the faith and to do so effectively.

When the Word of God goes out, it does not come back empty (Isaiah 55:11); you are not alone nor must you have the exactly right answer every time. God is going to do His work! There is a generation in need of the goodness of the Gospel. They are scraping to find meaning in life. Friendships, jobs, and a long line of relationships have let them down. But the Gospel will not. This is the importance of what you have to share; this is why it is important to earn your voice. Scripture says, "Walk in wisdom toward outsiders, making the best use of the time. Let your speech always be gracious, seasoned with salt, so that you may know how you ought to answer each person" (Colossians 4:5–6). Earning your voice is just that. It is gaining wisdom in how to be gracious in your speech.

Earning your voice is about having a chance to share the Gospel.

There are two classic approaches to use when sharing the Gospel: telling someone what to believe, and another that can be summed up as "Preach the Gospel, use words if necessary." There is a tension between these two ideas, especially when connecting with Millennials in an attempt to share the Gospel message with them.

As Christians, it can be easy for us to forget how much people need to hear the Gospel. Too often our modus operandi is simply telling people they are sinners. Maybe we don't go about it using such direct words, but instead of kind and gracious talk coming out of our mouths, we move straight to "tough love."

Let's mention a few quick points:

» When the Word of God goes out, it doesn't come back empty.

» As Christians, we are called to proclaim the Gospel to those around us.

» God is at work around you. You are not alone.

Our goal is not to defend God. It is to proclaim the Gospel. Our need for the Gospel is shown to us in light of the Law. What we are not saying is that you should ignore the failings of the world that would draw us farther away from Jesus. No. Instead we are pointing out that many Millennials believe that the Church only talks loudest about our moral imperatives. To the outside world, it seems as if on Sunday we proclaim Christ crucified, the greatest love the world has ever known, and the rest of the week we try to tell people how to live. How do we tackle this? The world will be antagonistic toward us

> **Our goal is not to defend God. It is to proclaim the Gospel.**

because of the Gospel message. Jesus promised us that. But do we want them to be antagonistic toward us because we have lost the ability to communicate respectfully? We speak the truth in love (Ephesians 4:15). We know there is such a thing as tough love. But we must realize that there is a difference between being a jerk and speaking the truth in love. Relationship, once again, is key. Do you know the person well enough to speak to them a hard truth? Think back to our talk about having a Law-and-Gospel worldview. Sometimes people are unrepentant and need that truth that convicts them. But make sure you are the right person to convict. It has to be a balance. You have to live in the tension.

Witnessing to Millennials outside the Church

Regaining gentleness and kindness is key to our witness to Millennials. Again, these concepts are not our own invention. Sometimes, looking for the "new answer" causes us to overlook the one already there in Scripture:

> » Remind them to be submissive to rulers and authorities, to be obedient, to be ready for every good work, to speak evil of no one, to avoid quarreling, to be gentle, and to show perfect courtesy toward all people. For we ourselves were once foolish, disobedient, led astray, slaves to various passions and pleasures, passing our days in malice and envy, hated by others and hating one another. But when the goodness and loving kindness of God our Savior appeared, He saved us, not because of works done by us in righteousness, but according to His own mercy, by the washing of regeneration and renewal of the Holy Spirit, whom He poured out on us richly through Jesus Christ our Savior, so that being justified by His grace we might become heirs according to the hope of eternal life. (Titus 3:1–7)

> » But in your hearts honor Christ the Lord as holy, always being prepared to make a defense to anyone who asks you for a reason for the hope that is in you; yet do it with gentleness and respect. (1 Peter 3:15)

> » Brothers, if anyone is caught in any transgression, you who are spiritual should restore him in a spirit of gentleness. Keep watch on yourself, lest you too be tempted. (Galatians 6:1)

> » Know this, my beloved brothers: let every person be quick to hear, slow to speak, slow to anger; for the anger of man does not produce the righteousness of God. (James 1:19–20)

> » But as for you, O man of God, flee these things. Pursue righteousness, godliness, faith, love, steadfastness, gentleness. (1 Timothy 6:11)

» Put on then, as God's chosen ones, holy and beloved, compassionate hearts, kindness, humility, meekness, and patience, bearing with one another and, if one has a complaint against another, forgiving each other; as the Lord has forgiven you, so you also must forgive. And above all these put on love, which binds everything together in perfect harmony. And let the peace of Christ rule in your hearts, to which indeed you were called in one body. And be thankful. (Colossians 3:12–15)

» Be kind to one another, tenderhearted, forgiving one another, as God in Christ forgave you. (Ephesians 4:32)

» But love your enemies, and do good, and lend, expecting nothing in return, and your reward will be great, and you will be sons of the Most High, for He is kind to the ungrateful and the evil. (Luke 6:35)

» A man who is kind benefits himself, but a cruel man hurts himself. (Proverbs 11:17)

The Hebrew word *hesed* is found often in the Old Testament. It refers to one thing: God's love for us. It is often translated as "steadfast love" or "loving kindness." Our God has a loving kindness for us that knows no bounds. No matter how far we have strayed, no matter how much we seek to destroy the vestige of Him in our daily lives, He chases after us. He loves us with a loving kindness that knows no bounds. If God has granted so much for us, why do we seem to so quickly want to be unkind in our dealings with outsiders?

In conversations with Millennials, this topic came up again and again: "How can the Church possibly be trustworthy? Look how they treat people!" Chelsey and I have found that the more we sought to earn our voices with Millennials, the more they heard us—even on issues of the Law. Millennials were more open to hearing about disagreements when, instead of simply telling them "how it is," we had first spent time showing them that we had voices worth listening to. This isn't some self-aggrandizing gimmick. "Look at Chelsey and me and how great we are!" This comes from lessons learned after one too many times of us shoving our feet so far into our mouths surgery would be required for removal. Okay, I am mainly referring to myself, but still.

Instead of seeking to be right and justified by our stand for truth, we, as Christians, must instead speak the truth with kindness. Why? Because Jesus became the truth for us. We are no different from anyone else on this planet, save one thing: we know that the work, death, and resurrection of Jesus was accomplished for us and all sinners. The salvation Jesus earned for us also enables us to earn our voices.

But what about our actions? Won't people just know we are Christians by our love? The answer is yes, but it is only a partial answer. The phrase "Preach the Gospel, use words if necessary" is attributed to St. Francis of Assisi. This quote floats around and has several different variations, but it creates a false dichotomy. The idea that the Gospel need only be taught through our actions is a false one. Why? Because St. Paul tells us, "So faith comes from hearing, and hearing through the word of Christ" (Romans 10:17). We must be ready to use words to tell the story of Jesus, to proclaim the Gospel. This is why earning your voice is so important. The works done as a Christian help us to earn our voice with people. That voice declares the Word of the Lord for them. And His Word does not go out without power.

PRACTICAL STEPS

> **The works done as a Christian help us to earn our voice with people. That voice declares the Word of the Lord for them.**

What then are some practical steps for earning your voice? Glad you asked!

There are so many different ways that you could tackle this, but we want to share the three most important: empathy, belonging over being right, and policing your social media.

Empathy

Empathy goes an incredibly long way in helping you earn your voice with the Millennial generation. At times, it feels like no matter what we say, no one hears us. No matter how many times we talk about our crippling school debt, our inability to get jobs, or how insane the housing market has become, we are simply dismissed with the wave of a hand and a muttered, "Millennials."

But what if empathy became the new normal? Instead of scoffing at us and believing every news report, sit down with a Millennial and say, "That must be tough." Instead of belittling our pain and struggle, take a moment to step into it with us. Some of it will be stupid, the ramblings of young people finding their way in the world. But weren't you once a young person trying to find your way in this world? It's not that we need you to fix everything for us. We just need you to empathize and see that it might be harder than you thought to be a part of this "entitled" generation.

Belonging over Being Right

As humans, we have a deep need to be right. Maybe that would be better phrased as a deep insecurity that expresses itself by the need to be right. When it comes to communication, this need manifests itself when we constantly tell other people why they are wrong. Let us tell you something we have learned about Millennials from living in their midst our whole lives: being right does not earn your voice as much as allowing people to belong. Often we have sat across the table from people we strongly disagree with, but what we have learned is that being their friends affords us a chance to speak the truth. But only if we lose our need to be right.

Sometimes, this manifests itself as trying to defend God. This is the Lord of the armies and hosts of heaven we are talking about. He probably has defense of Himself covered. What if instead of seeking our own rightness we instead seek to understand? We are not saying do not speak the truth, but instead earn the right to speak the truth. Show someone they belong before you rush to show them how they are wrong.

Police Your Social Media

We remember when Facebook was just for college kids. When it opened up to the public, there was weeping and gnashing of teeth at universities across the country. Instead of Facebook being ours, now our parents, our little brothers and sisters, and our grandparents were on Facebook. That was a watershed moment. From there we got Twitter, LinkedIn, and Instagram.

What also came at that watershed moment was a large influx of the ability to share whatever you thought about whatever you were thinking. Facebook has changed immensely over the past several years. It used to be a picture of you and your wall. You couldn't share links as easily; there was no Facebook live, or even picture albums. But when Facebook began rolling out to everyone, it began transforming in all kinds of ways, adding extra capabilities. It became a place for news, opinions, and creating an online persona. Instantly sharing your views and thoughts on any subject under the sun became the new norm. The question is, should you?

Want to have a voice with Millennials? Social media posts from older generations is a core complaint among people our age. "Did you see what they posted?!" In this arena of social media, you can lose credibility incredibly quickly. What we are not saying is you should not post anything. But when you do, try and look at it from another person's point of view. Remember that on social media you lose the ability to interact face-to-face. Don't lose your voice by posting on social media in anger or frustration. Take time to look at an idea from all angles. If you still wish to post it, do it, but make sure that if it is controversial you move forward in kindness and gentleness. Also, know that it is okay to NOT post something on social media. Especially if it is a something that starts with "Say this prayer in the next five minutes . . . " and ends with " . . . share it with 5 friends and you will be blessed!" Just say no to spam posting.

MILLENNIALS, A WORD ON SOCIAL MEDIA . . .

Police.

Your.

Social.

Media.

This sword cuts two ways. Don't use social media to tear others apart. Let's stop posting about how bad we have it. Also, your partying on spring break five years ago is probably not your proudest moment. It might be time to pull those pictures down. But let us not become a generation who blames other generations for our own faults. Articles and posts that only tear down older generations while giving the reasons why problems x, y, and z are not our fault are not helpful to the growth of our generation nor to the betterment of society as a whole.

Gaining a voice with older generations means putting in our time. Don't show up at the table thinking you are God's gift to humanity. I can say that because I've done it. I've believed my own press. It never ends well for me. It is important for us to put in our time, to let our hard work speak for who we are. Ask good questions. Instead of trying to force your solution to every problem or think your idea is the one that will finally reveal the truth behind unicorns, ask good questions. Try it for a couple of weeks. In church. At work. With your family. Ask good questions.

Then—this will be novel—listen. Our generation has been incredibly blessed. There have been wars, but none that have called away our entire generation. We have experienced a recession, but not one that would recall the breadlines of the Great Depression. We wouldn't be here today if it wasn't for the great cloud of witnesses (Hebrews 12:1) who came before us. It is good for us to listen. To hear the stories and wisdom of those who went before us. The more we listen, the more we show that we are still learning, the more we earn a voice at the table with the older generations.

EARNING OUR VOICE

To the older generations, thank you. Thank you for reading this book. That alone shows that you have a desire for our generation to be connected with Jesus. Earning your voice is one step in that process. But we implore you, don't stop. Let your leadership be one that my generation seeks to reflect. Earn Millennial respect, not because you have to, but because with it you are offered the opportunity to share Jesus with people, to encourage those already in the Body of Christ, and to bring hope to those who do not yet know Him.

MILLENNIALS, LET'S RESPECT . . .

Let us be a generation who seeks to respect those who came before us. By picking up this book you have a heart for your generation too. Yet, you also have a heart for the generations ahead of you. Let that shine through. Let us respect those who came before us because they have so much to offer us. Seek out ways to honor your elders. Ask good questions; be quick to listen and slow to speak. Also, give them insight into your friends and co-workers, people your age. Help them see the Millennial generation.

In earning our voice, the words of James must ring true in our ears:

So also the tongue is a small member, yet it boasts of great things. How great a forest is set ablaze by such a small fire! And the tongue is a fire, a world of unrighteousness. The tongue is set among our members, staining the whole body, setting on fire the entire course of life, and set on fire by hell. For every kind of beast and bird, of reptile and sea creature, can be tamed and has been tamed by mankind, but no human being can tame the tongue. It is a restless evil, full of deadly poison. With it we bless our Lord and Father, and with it we curse people who are made in the likeness of God. From the same mouth come blessing and cursing. My brothers, these things ought not to be so. . . . But the wisdom from above is first pure, then peaceable, gentle, open to reason, full of mercy and good fruits, impartial and sincere. And a harvest of righteousness is sown in peace by those who make peace. (James 3:5–10, 17–18)

DISCUSSION QUESTIONS

1. What do you think about the idea of earning your voice?

2. Older generations—Do you see any ways that your leadership reflects the attitude of the Millennials?

3. Millennials—Do you struggle with respecting people in the older generations? Why?

4. Why might it be difficult to show gentleness and kindness in the process of earning your voice?

5. Why is the Gospel important for you?

6. What are some practical ways you can work on earning your voice in your life?

DO IT

If you are doing this in a group with mixed generations, take some time and share ways that you think they could earn their voice with people in your generation. (If you're not in a group, don't worry, we've got you covered: go to someone you trust in a generation different from you and ask the same question.)

THE LUTHERAN OPPORTUNITY

Ted

Now, this is a book written by a Lutheran couple for a Lutheran publishing house, which means it's a safe bet that a majority of you reading it are Lutheran. Now, if you aren't, that's okay too.[21] This chapter focuses on some aspects of Lutheranism that connect well with the Millennial generation.

Let's dive in.

LAW AND GOSPEL

Ashlee and I have been friends since middle school. We grew up at the same church and went to the same high school. Ashlee ended up marrying one of our best friends from college, Jon. When we got the call to plant a church right out of seminary, and after celebrating the occasion with our families, Jon and Ashlee were our first call. We asked them a

---

21 Want to learn more about Lutherans? Check out *The Genius of Luther's Theology* by Robert Kolb and Charles Arand and *Being Lutheran* by A. Trevor Sutton.

simple question: would you leave the life you have built in Houston to join us on the adventure of planting a church north of Austin? There were months of prayer and wrestling over the decision, but in the summer of 2015, Jon and Ashlee joined us. We have been laboring together in this work since.

One of the great joys I have had in leading alongside my friends is sharing a deeper understanding of our Lutheran worldview. Ashlee and I have had some amazing conversations around several different topics, but none greater than looking at the world through the lens of Law and Gospel. We've had some fun conversations around the biblical view of Law and Gospel. We have even discussed how Law and Gospel can be used to see the world we live in and how to engage with it.

I will never forget the day this really hit home for Ashlee. We were talking about an interaction she had with a friend, and she looked at me and said, "They just really needed the Gospel." Boom. There it was. A friend of mine applying Law and Gospel in her daily life.

Law and Gospel as Doctrine

It is important for us to understand that, foundationally, Law and Gospel is a way we view the Bible. By separating Scripture into the Law, that which condemns us of sin and calls us to righteous living, and Gospel, the saving work of Jesus for us and all sinners, we avoid the trap of falling into works-righteousness, the belief that our salvation comes through the things we do. The doctrine of Law and Gospel, this teaching of the Lutheran Church, is central to how we operate as a church. In it, we are given a key way of interpreting Scripture.

Remember when we talked in chapter 3 about Millennials' struggle with failure? the need to always be perfect that Millennials struggle with daily? Law and Gospel counters that struggle. The Law reminds us that we cannot be perfect on our own. The Gospel tells us that we don't need to be because Jesus is. In His death and resurrection, He places His "perfectness" on us. Instead of a faith based on seeking to be perfect, Christianity is imperfect people being perfected by the perfect sacrifice of Jesus. The law is a lens through which the stark reality of the world is revealed; there is no way to attain the perfection for which we strive. Failure can serve as a harsh reminder of humanity's sinful nature, but it is not an end! We do not have to remain in despair because this painful moment of clarity opens the door to finding comfort in the Gospel: the only perfection we need is that offered by the soothing words of the Savior, "Neither do I condemn you; go, and . . . sin no more" (John 8:11).

It is easy to try to guilt people into following Jesus. All you have to do is tell people how sinful and broken they are. Sell them the insurance of "turn or burn." But to a generation already skeptical of the institutional Church, the fire and balm of Law and Gospel is revolutionary. We can share the detriment of sin; in fact, I have found in my preaching that Millennials more readily accept the hard teachings of the Law. But Christians cannot assume people know the Gospel. Every chance we get, every moment we have an opportunity in front of someone, from the pulpit or on the driveway, let us proclaim that Jesus is for people. Law and Gospel is not about condemnation. It is about the reality of sin in our lives and the joy that can be found only in our Savior. Law and Gospel as a doctrine and understanding of Scripture will connect with Millennials because it helps them understand how God can coexist as a God of both wrath and love.

Law and Gospel is not about condemnation. It is about the reality of sin in our lives and the joy that can be found only in our Savior.

Law and Gospel as Worldview

Theology and doctrine are great because they don't occur only as existential ideas; they are tools that help the Christian navigate everyday life. This was mentioned in chapter 2. The Lutheran understanding of Law and Gospel can combat perceptions of Millennial laziness or feelings of anxiety. There are numerous applications for looking at our world through this lens. How can we tell if someone needs the quick hammer of the Law or the soothing waters of the Gospel? Look at how they are acting. Are they unrepentant, self-centered, and hard-hearted? This person is in need of that hammer, but in kindness. But if they are repentant, seeing their sin for what it is, this person needs the Gospel. They need to hear that there is a Savior who took the full blow of the Law for them.

As you connect with Millennials, this understanding of Law and Gospel might be the greatest tool in your box. It will be easy to become frustrated or angry, to look at young people and see only the stereotypes. But what if you applied a Law and Gospel lens to those relationships? It would change everything. Instead of seeing Millennials as solely being lazy, entitled snowflakes, you might see that there is sin and fear in their lives, buried deep below the surface. The Lutheran understanding of Law and Gospel allows us to approach relationships with compassion. Instead of seeking to transform people, we gently bring the Law in to show them that life is more than what they are living. The Gospel works as a soothing balm, hope to the hopeless.

What if we could all do this for one another? Generations seeking to bring Law and Gospel, conviction and healing, to the other?

MILLENNIALS, QUICK SIDEBAR . . .

There are things we simply do not understand in the same way that the Gen Xers and Boomers do. They have seen things and experienced life in many incredible and different ways. Applying Law and Gospel to our lives allows us to seek compassion and humility instead of seeking a need to be right or justified. Let's throw away our victim card, which often hinders our ability to love, and instead seek to see older generations in the way Jesus sees them.

There are things you simply do not understand in the same way that Millennials do. But a Law and Gospel approach allows us to seek life together. Instead of focusing on what is wrong with one another, we seek to grow as disciples together. That is something Millennials are seeking, an authentic community that cares deeply enough for one another to love them and still call them to hope.

Justification and Sanctification

Here is another clear Lutheran doctrine that cuts deeply to the heart of the Millennial: justification and sanctification. Martin Luther's great joy was to be able to tell those around him that there was nothing they could do to gain their salvation, *but* it was their God-given duty to love their neighbor. You might ask, who is my neighbor? Yes. That is the answer I give to that question whenever anyone asks it. If you are asking, "Is this person my neighbor?" Yes. "But I really don't want them to be my neighbor." Tough. Anyone you have a connection with is your neighbor, whether it is your literal neighbor or the person around the world who needs your help. The clear distinction of justification and sanctification is at the core of the Lutheran ethos. And it is a distinction our generation desperately needs to understand.

A Quick Story

My brother and I had been attending a nondenominational mission conference together. Unfortunately, I had to leave early to get home, but I later asked my brother how the conference had ended. Dejectedly, he told me that the last speaker made a point with which he couldn't agree. Intrigued, I asked him to explain. He told me that the speaker had pleaded with the conference to have a passion for mission, locally and internationally. Then this speaker threw the right hook. The exact wording has left me over time, but the gist of his point was this: if you don't have a passion for missions and lost people, then you need to question whether you have been saved. Overall, this conference had been fairly good, but that one statement shot a torpedo through the whole thing.

Millennials have heard time and again, both warranted and unwarranted, that being a part of the Body of Christ means you *must* behave a certain way. To be a part of the family you *must* have your act together. This flies in the face of the distinction between justification and sanctification. The justification of Christ for us is an alien righteousness. It is a work that we cannot do. It is bringing the dead to life. There is no way that we can do or be better to deserve justification. Our sins declare that we cannot.

But thankfully we know these things to be true:

> » Purge me with hyssop, and I shall be clean; wash me, and I shall be whiter than snow. (Psalm 51:7)

> » But He was pierced for our transgressions; He was crushed for our iniquities; upon Him was the chastisement that brought us peace, and with His wounds we are healed. (Isaiah 53:5)

> » For while we were still weak, at the right time Christ died for the ungodly. (Romans 5:6)

> » But He said to me, "My grace is sufficient for you, for My power is made perfect in weakness." Therefore I will boast all the more gladly of my weaknesses, so that the power of Christ may rest upon me. For the sake of Christ, then, I am content with weaknesses, insults, hardships, persecutions, and calamities. For when I am weak, then I am strong. (2 Corinthians 12:9–10)

> » The next day [John the Baptizer] saw Jesus coming toward him, and said, "Behold, the Lamb of God, who takes away the sin of the world!" (John 1:29)

Justification declares that salvation is a gift from outside ourselves. The Lutheran Church was born by confessing that in justification, "It is taught that we cannot obtain forgiveness of sin and righteousness before God through our merit, work, or satisfactions, but that we receive forgiveness of sin and become righteous before God out of grace for Christ's sake through faith when we believe that Christ has suffered for us and that for His sake our sin is forgiven and righteousness and eternal life are given to us" (Augsburg Confession, Article IV).[xx]

Jesus constantly tells people to go and sin no more, but what does that mean? It means that in our salvation, in the gift of life that Jesus has given us through His death and resurrection, we are called to more. All we needed from God was salvation. That could have been it. But instead, He gives us gift upon gift. Our sanctification is an ongoing process. It is a re-creation. The Holy Spirit is at work in our lives to re-create us to what

God originally intended humanity to be. In response to our unearned justification, we display our sanctification through our joy and by doing good
for others. Paul frames it for us this way: "For we are His workmanship,
created in Christ Jesus for good works, which God prepared beforehand,
that we should walk in them" (Ephesians 2:10). This process begins at
the moment of salvation and ends with the last breath of our mortal life.
But it is a continual process of learning one simple thing: Jesus' way is
better. Those same early Lutherans who confessed justification also confessed a life of new obedience in Article VI of the Augsburg Confession:
"It is also taught that such faith should yield good fruit and good works
and that a person must do such good works as God has commanded for
God's sake but not place trust in them as if thereby to earn grace before
God."xxi

When justification and sanctification are confused, the ramifications
on the life of a Christian can be far-reaching. Remember that Millennials
struggle with perfectionism. Another angle of that perfectionism is what
we might call destiny theology. In this worldview, God has a calling on
our lives to go and do big things, to fulfill our destinies. But what happens
when all we are doing is small things? Going to college, raising a family,
going to church, serving in our local communities. All of a sudden, Millennials feel this incredible amount of guilt that begins to root its way into our
hearts, about how we should be more missional or more relevant or more
liturgical or more impactful or more on fire. The list goes on and on, never
seeming to end. With this worldview, the goal of the Christian walk is not
to follow God in everyday living but to find a personal destiny.

But if we are not finding that destiny, we must not believe correctly.
We must not be doing what God has called us to do. Destiny theology is
another form of works-righteousness, and it has infected the Millennial
generation. There are destiny theologies in churches and destiny theologies in culture. Both have wriggled their way deep into the heart of the
Millennial psyche.

Justification and sanctification is freeing. It says that you do not have
to do anything to earn the favor of God. You already have it. Jesus didn't

die for some future, more obedient version of you. He died for you. But this salvation gives us a calling, another gift. One that says Jesus is better than our temptations. Sanctification is not a process of becoming more or less saved. Instead it is a journey of learning that when we sacrifice the things of this world for the ways of Jesus, it leads to our joy.

We love our neighbors. Not because our salvation depends on it, but because it is the way of Jesus.

We seek to end sinful behaviors in our life. Not because our salvation depends on it, but because the way of Jesus is better.

We want conviction of the Holy Spirit to work on hearts. We want to be re-created, because the way of Jesus is better.

THE MYSTERY OF THE SACRAMENTS

As we mentioned before, a majority of Millennials would fall somewhere in the range of being postmodern or premodern. Modernism falls around the idea that everything can be explained with reason or science. Modernism claims universal truths. Postmodernism is a reaction to modernism. It argues that "universal truths" are simply societal constructs. Postmodernism thus allows for relativism and pluralism. While detrimental in many ways, this mind-set does allow for mystery. Postmodernism gives Christians a chance to connect with Millennials concerning the Sacraments in an incredible way.

This does not mean the Sacraments should be taken lightly. But the teaching and importance of the Sacraments connect well with Millennials because of the mystery that surrounds them. A modern mind-set requires that we try to explain every piece of the puzzle, that we try to analyze our way into the in, with, and under-ness[22] of Holy Communion and the supernatural nature of Baptism. The Church needs that understanding—it is important to be able to articulate the Sacraments. But when connecting with and teaching Millennials, mystery is more readily accepted. It is okay

---

22   The phrase "in, with, and under" is the way Lutherans understand Jesus' physical nature as it is present in the Holy Sacraments.

to talk about the mystery of these Means of Grace, to talk about the wondrous mystery of our loving God who serves us in these ways.

A BURIED IDENTITY AND A BONDAGE OF THE WILL

We were buried therefore with Him by baptism into death, in order that, just as Christ was raised from the dead by the glory of the Father, we too might walk in newness of life. For if we have been united with Him in a death like His, we shall certainly be united with Him in a resurrection like His. (Romans 6:4–5)

Central to the Lutheran understanding of identity is Baptism. We often reference how our identity is buried with Christ. This comes straight from the Romans passage above. But why be so morbid? Because that is what we, as Lutheran Christians, truly believe. In our Baptism, we are buried, our old self goes into the water, drowned to death, and we come out as members of the family of God.

Culture is fighting for the identity of the Millennial generation. Will we only be as good as our stereotypes? Will we fall into the sinful traps that culture has placed for us? But Christians preach, teach, and confess an identity that cannot be stolen, that rust and moth do not destroy. A Christian's identity in Christ is so rooted in who he is that he had to die to receive it. Christians have to be buried beneath the water and the Word. But that new identity is ours. We are heirs of the kingdom of God. That is an identity worth talking about.

This identity doesn't come from something as fickle as our own reason, but instead from God Himself. Luther talks of a river and how it is bound by its banks. So, too, our will is bound by God. As the world tells us, that freedom is only about getting what is best for us. It says we should be offended when we don't get our way, or that we are entitled to more. But the bondage of our will in Christ transforms us. In this bondage the Holy Spirit first claims us. Through this bondage we are given salvation and new life. Being bound to the will of God gives us a clarity we could not hope for on our own. We are shown that our goal is not to become the greatest but is instead to become the least. The treasures of this life do not hold sway over us because we seek first the kingdom of God.

The Lutheran understanding of identity is strong. It is an asset for Christians in connecting with all generations, especially this Millennial generation. Identity is being pulled in every direction for our generation. Idols are constantly seeking to grow in importance, and Millennials are seeking identities for themselves to feel like they belong.

AUTHENTICITY

As Chelsey said in chapter 7, if there is one phrase you will hear over and over from Millennials, it is that they desire authenticity. As Lutherans, we should strive for authenticity in who we are. There are a few great ways—the church calendar, liturgical elements, and lamenting—in which we do this. As we connect with new people, we need to be ready to teach them the importance of what is second nature to us.

The Church Calendar

Lutherans have observed the liturgical Church calendar for many generations. Some congregations are more likely than others to celebrate minor feast days or festivals. But the seasons of Advent, Christmas, Lent, Holy Week, Easter, Pentecost, and so on are widely celebrated in our churches. This is a testament to who we are. The liturgical calendar gives the Church a rhythm in which to follow Jesus—a yearly reminder that we are His and, as His people, we remember His life and His work for our salvation.

The Lord's Prayer, the Creeds, and Congregational Singing

Somewhere along the line this phrase became vogue: "We don't want to just be going through the motions." In some ways, this is true even in our lives as Christians. Faith should not be built on simply repetitively doing the same thing over and over. The life of the Church is not simply a rote checklist of what we need to do, because then we move from being the Church to being a cult. Instead, we say the Lord's Prayer, recite the Creeds, and sing hymns and songs so that when we are in deep distress or our faculties fail us toward the end of life, we are still able to remember the promises of Jesus.

When we go to visit my Grandma Doering in the nursing home, we are lucky if she remembers us. She usually gets her children right and once in a while I see that she remembers me. Grandma is able to get about three sentences out before the Alzheimer's disease kicks in and she becomes incoherent. If not for the Church and our Savior, visiting Grandma would only be depressing. Instead, there is hope. I have watched Grandma sing songs to my nieces, her great-granddaughters. I have listened to her confess the Apostles' Creed word for word from memory. And I have been privileged to close every visit with her with the Lord's Prayer, all of which she knows. She knows all these things because she grew up with them. It is not going through the motions if it is the way we can remember the promises of Jesus. Instead, it is the joy of having the words of God written on our hearts.

Millennials are interested in the kinds of things that last. Their grandparents are in the nursing home. They ask themselves when they will begin taking care of their own parents. But what an exclamation of hope to a generation who has lost their way. Even when their minds have wandered, the faith remains.

We cannot lose our heritage. There must be some way for us as Lutherans to share it with the next generation while not becoming irrelevant. If the decision is made that our heritage is a part of a club, some kind of secret society that you can only enter with the right behavior or the correct turn of phrase, we have lost what the reformers fought so hard for years ago. The relevancy Lutherans bring to the table is not that we are cool, but that we love to teach. Repetitive teaching is our game. But not simply repetition for repetition's sake. No. Repetition for the sake of our constant need to be reminded of the goodness of God for His creation. That He would send Jesus for us. Our teaching must always facilitate that the promises of Jesus move from our heads to our hearts, from our hearts to our hands. If we stop taking the time to teach Christ crucified in meaningful ways for everyday people, we have lost our way and will fall into irrelevancy.

Confession and Absolution

Accountability has become a major part of American Christianity. Often meeting in groups or partners, people are searching for ways to battle the sins that entrap them. I have found one aspect is often missing from this process: confession and absolution.

As Lutherans, we acknowledge that any good we receive comes from God. If this is true, then the power to resist sin does not come from some amped-up self-discipline. Instead, it flows from the forgiveness we receive from our Savior. Again and again, people are tempted into thinking that Jesus will love them more if they are just a little bit more obedient. Confession and absolution remind us that Jesus loves us where we are. His saving power, given to us by the Holy Spirit, enables us to follow Him. We are going to fall short, but absolution assures us that Jesus will not abandon us because we make mistakes. Scripture tells us, "Confess your sins to one another and pray for one another, that you may be healed. The prayer of a righteous person has great power as it is working" (James 5:16). Start this process yourself. Maybe it is in a formal setting with a pastor, or maybe it is informal with a brother or sister in Christ, but power to resist sin does not come from self-discipline. It comes from the forgiveness given to us in Jesus.

Millennials have seen all the self-help gurus, from Oprah to their psych professor. Let's show them that self is not what heals; instead, it is walking in humility before God by confessing our failings and receiving His forgiveness time and again.

MILLENNIALS, MY BROTHERS AND SISTERS . . .

. . . find a confession and absolution partner. As we grew up, there was a craze for accountability partners. I encourage you to find someone you can confess to, someone with whom you can admit the sin in your life. When we confess our sin, it brings it to light, it keeps us from hiding it. Then we can experience the deep forgiveness Jesus has won for us. Find someone to be this person with you, who will hear your confession and proclaim the promises of Jesus to you and for you. I do this with my kid brother. It is amazing to let someone else hear my sin, but then to hear how Jesus washed those things away. Our willpower will not make us better followers of Jesus. The power of the Gospel in our lives does that.

Lamenting

Lutherans have not lost the ability to lament; Millennials will connect with that. They live in a world that no longer creates *Leave It to Beaver* but instead produces *Game of Thrones*, *The Walking Dead*, and *Breaking Bad*, television shows that instead of wrapping up everything happily in thirty minutes, spend seasons ripping the heart out of their audience in visceral ways—many times through the deaths of beloved characters or a seemingly nonchalant view of death. Millennials consume news media at the fastest rate of any generation before them because news travels in seconds. We do not have rose-colored glasses. We have seen the world through unfiltered social media and have become jaded. We don't want to be told that everything will be all right because we have seen that it won't be. Being happy all the time is not an option for us. But lamenting allows for this. It shows that even in the darkness, the light is coming. It acknowledges the reality of the world but proclaims the hope of Jesus.

MILLENNIALS, FOR THE LOVE OF THE CHURCH, LAMENT.

Lament for the tragedies in this world. Lament for your friends who are leaving the Church. Lament for the evil that is happening in and around you. Lament when friends lose a child, when cancer strikes another person, when the culture is against Jesus. Lamenting is a gift from God, a way for us to express our very human emotions and release our anxieties, fears, and angers to a God who loves us.

JESUS

The greatest opportunity that we have as Lutherans is to preach Christ crucified. Our heritage is translating the Bible into the language of the common tongue so that all could learn about God's free gift of grace through reading Scripture or hearing the Gospel purely preached.

That is still true today. What Lutherans can offer a generation who is walking away from the Church is Jesus. Many man-made bandages have been used to try to slow the departure of young people from the Church. All along our greatest weapon was Jesus.

That is the point of this entire book.

The world has clumped Millennials into set stereotypes and personas, trying to sell them the Church by using marketing tactics or sociological studies. But the truth of the matter is that they are all individuals. They will fit into many of these categories, but not every person will fit. And that is good. Because we are not trying to save people with sociology or marketing. Jesus is saving people with His Church.

When we focus solely on increasing church membership, we have lost sight of the mission of the kingdom of God. In Luke 15, Jesus tells the story of the prodigal son. The younger son demands his inheritance early and squanders what he receives. The older son is jealous and angry that he remained obedient, while his brother spent his money on prostitutes. Yet their father celebrates his younger brother. But do you know what is the same for both of these brothers? Their father comes out to them.

The father runs to embrace the younger brother.

The father leaves the party to talk to the moping older brother.

There is only—and can ever be only—one hope for the Millennial generation. It is the hope of the Builders, the Busters, the Boomers, and the Xers. Jesus only can ever be that hope. Introducing people to Him is our goal. Jesus tells us time and again it is His joy to seek and to save the lost:

> And when he comes home, he calls together his friends and his neighbors, saying to them, "Rejoice with me, for I have found my sheep that was lost." . . . And when she has found it, she calls together her friends and neighbors, saying, "Rejoice with me, for I have found the coin that I had lost." . . . "For this my son was dead, and is alive again; he was lost, and is found." And they began to celebrate. . . . "It was fitting to celebrate and be glad, for this your brother was dead, and is alive; he was lost, and is found." (Luke 15:6, 9, 24, 32)
>
> For the Son of Man came to seek and to save the lost. (Luke 19:10)

It is the joy of the King to seek out the lost. If we are in the Kingdom, we seek to be like the King. How amazing would it have been had the older brother dropped what he was doing in the field to run out and meet his younger brother with his father?

The opportunity to do just that is before us. Let us be the Church Militant, walking out into a hostile world, carrying the banner of the King. God has uniquely set His people up to reach this generation in some incredible ways. It is our joy to serve Him, for He is the hope of the world.

Discussion Questions

1. How does the Lutheran understanding of Law and Gospel inform your reading of Scripture? How does it work in your life?

2. What is the importance of the Sacraments in your life?

3. Have you ever thought of yourself as being buried with Christ in your Baptism? What does that mean for you on a daily basis?

4. How can you honor your brothers and sisters in Christ?

5. Who in your life needs to hear about Jesus?

Do It

Confess and be absolved. Go to your pastor or a trusted brother or sister in Christ. Repent your sins bare, and hear the proclamation of forgiveness through Jesus!

PRACTICAL ADVICE FOR ORGANIZATIONS

Ted

You did it. Ten chapters. If we could high-five you in person we would, but if you want to get a digital one, just head over to giphy.com and search "high five." Consider that a gift from us. We have told you stories of real Millennials to give faces and names to a group of people reduced to stereotypes and statistics. We've asked you to consider mentoring Millennials, building relationships with them, and inviting them into community with you. At this point, Chelsey and I must reiterate that we believe the Millennial generation will connect with the Gospel in those ways—when they hear you share the message of Jesus Christ in the contexts of mentorship, relationship, and community.

However, we would be remiss if we didn't spend a small amount of time describing how organizations, especially churches, can practically connect with Millennials. We've spent ten chapters expounding on relationships, mentoring, and community, and just one on practical methods. This was a deliberate disproportion on our part—for it's more important to understand generational differences than it is to provide you with the "silver bullet" for connecting with Millennials. Mostly because silver bullets never really work, and because we know that every context is different.

In this chapter, we focus on how your church can be more attractive versus trying to be attractional. The difference between these two is easy. Think of it this way: how do you get your house ready for guests to come over? If it's a standing dinner, like a weekly evening meal with friends or family, you'll do normal things like make the beds, sweep, maybe do some mopping, clean the bathrooms, maybe even mow the lawn. But a few times each year, for those really special events, you'll add a bit of deep cleaning to your preparations. You might throw down some new mulch, plant some new plants, fertilize the yard to make it extra green, and power-wash the driveway and back patio. Then, there are the big projects: a deck, planting a new garden, building a new fence. You do all of these things to maintain the value of your house, but you also do them so that when guests come over you can welcome them into a clean, inviting, and warm environment.

What you aren't doing is adding a Ferris wheel.[23]

In our homes, we don't often add attractions. Some folks may have a pool or a media room, but most of the time, we want our homes to be *attractive* so that people feel welcomed when they come over to visit. This is what our organizations need to be doing. We won't ask you to add any attractions. Instead, we want to propose some housekeeping ideas that you can easily implement so that when people come for a visit or check out your online presence, they see an attractive and inviting atmosphere.

Our focus will be on the Church. However, these ideas will also work well with other organizations. These are not holy or religious ideas; they are just some tips for helping people from the outside looking in to see your organization in the best light—especially when it comes to Millennials.

---

23   If you are adding a Ferris wheel to your house, please invite us over for dinner.

SPEAKING OF WHICH . . . MILLENNIALS, OVER HERE . . .

Here is what I know. Not all of you are social media wizards. Not all of you know how to build a website. But whatever skills you do have, help in these areas—especially if you do have some knowledge of social media and websites. Help your churches with these things. Encourage them as they grow in learning how to use these new media for fostering outreach and making connections.

TIDYING UP YOUR IMAGE

Many churches break the cardinal rule of simpler being better, or less is more. Churches often make things too complicated: they try to cram as much information in people's faces as they can. From bulletins to websites, churches often want people to see *everything* going on at first glance. What this does is clutter your image. Imagine it this way: if, in your home, you put all your keepsakes, family photos, furniture, and heirlooms in the living room, you would probably be accused of being a hoarder. However, when those things are spread throughout the house with a little bit of consideration of interior design, it is not overwhelming. In fact, those things function to make your house hospitable.

Let's work on some things that can help clean up your image.

Fonts

All right. Repeat after me: I will *never* use Papyrus or Comic Sans again. These two fonts are the most overused fonts on the face of the planet. Papyrus is used to make things look old and weathered. Comic Sans is used to make people think you are in the 1960s version of *Batman*. Either way, they communicate one thing: "We are not professional."

At one time, it was considered groundbreaking for these two fonts to grace the pages of all kinds of bulletins, announcements, and projector screens. These fonts brought with them the opportunity to get away from the traditional typewriter font. Well, that time has passed. In fact, we encourage you to bury these two fonts out back with as much haste as possible.

"Why do you even care about fonts?" Glad you asked! Remember, this isn't about deep substance; this is about creating a welcoming environment. Papyrus and Comic Sans immediately communicate that you are out of touch with the rest of the modern world. Go look at popular advertising, publications, and websites. No one uses these fonts anymore. Instead, designers and advertisers alike are opting for either a more defined block font or something that appears handwritten. The best option would be to pick one clean font—we recommend Helvetica or Calibri—and stick with it.

There will likely be a time when Comic Sans and Papyrus return to vogue, just like bell-bottoms and wallpaper. But for now, exorcise them from your computers.

Try to find one or two main fonts to use in your publications. Keeping things uniform with a clean font like Helvetica or Calibri is the best way to go. Instead of trying to make a splash, try to make things clean. Millennial communication styles veer toward clean over busy, straightforward over complex.

"But what if I NEED a font to make a splash?" No problem! There are some great resources for that.

- **www.fontsquirrel.com**—Check out this website. It has tons of free fonts that you can use if you are making something that doesn't bring in a profit. In fact, each font will tell you exactly what it is licensed for under its terms of usage.

- **www.creativemarket.com**—If you are looking for a specialized font for publication, Creative Market is the place to go. When you sign up for a login, they will send you an email every Monday with six free downloads, from fonts and graphics to wallpapers and design elements.

"How will I know when and how to use these fonts?" All right, overachiever. Stop getting ahead of us. We're getting there.

Clip Art

Stop it. Just . . . don't.

You don't want to use clip art. I don't want you to use clip art. Millennials don't want you to use clip art.

So don't use clip art.

Once again, this communicates that you are behind the times. The truth? You don't need to be! Instead, opt for clean. Instead of using clip art, stick to good fonts and clean text. Clip art filled a great void when not everyone had access to great graphics. The good news is that you, too, can make great graphics.

Put down the clip art and work on incorporating graphics.

What is a graphic? It can be a lot of things.

What isn't it? Clip art. Graphics usually incorporate some type of stylized font connected to an image. Sometimes they just involve fonts. Some churches out there may be able to hire someone to handle their graphic design needs for them while others cannot.

But here's the good news: making graphics has become so much simpler in our day and age. Find good resources, pay for what you can, but know that there are many free options out there. Here are some resources I recommend:

- **www.unsplash.com**—Free stock photos. Unsplash is a collective of photographers who offer up their photos free for commercial use, which means you can use them for free. There are some amazing photos in there, all of which are searchable. At my church, we use this on a weekly basis for graphics.

- **www.kaboompics.com**—Similar to Unsplash, with a different selection of photos.

- **www.freelyphotos.com**—Another free-commercial-use stock photo site. Freely, however, specifically focuses on Christian photos.

- **Photoshop**—Adobe has been the go-to graphic editor for years. In the past, Photoshop was an incredibly expensive program, but now you can buy a monthly subscription for about the same price as a month of Netflix. For a little extra, you can get the entire Adobe suite, which includes things like Publisher and Illustrator. This is a professional program and will have a learning curve, but if you can spend the time learning, you will produce your own great graphics in no time!

- **www.canva.com**—Canva is an online graphics editor. This is great for beginners or people who want to produce graphics but don't have the time to learn a professional program. Canva offers free membership, or you can pay each month to gain access to more features.

- **Word Swag**—An app that allows you to add text to photos easily. There is a free version, but you can unlock the full version for a couple of bucks. I use this each week to put together a quick Instagram post containing a thought for that Sunday's sermon. It has now been updated to allow you to choose between Instagram, Twitter, and Facebook for specific dimensions of posts.

- **www.prochurchtools.com**—Pro Church Tools was started several years ago in Toronto by a man named Brady Shearer. This company works to help churches grow in their ability to use the tools around them to create a better image. You can sign up and pay for different packages. Options include hiring them to produce content for you, or simply using your email to get some free tutorials. I had to wear the hat of graphic designer at our church for several years, and I learned a lot from the tutorials and tips from Pro Church Tools.

Website

Repeat after me: "This is our new church sign." The first thing people see of you, a majority of the time, is your website. At one time, many moons ago, there was the belief that every piece of information you have should go on the front page so people can find it faster. Today, however, we live in a day and age where people have learned to navigate websites. Dismiss the "everything on the front page" notion from your minds. Strike it from your vocabulary. Instead, put the most important information on your front page and learn to love the ability to link people to other pages.

Make sure you have a calendar, and make sure that calendar is kept up-to-date. This is something we can say because we, as our church, have been the greatest perpetrators. When people land on your website, it is important for them to know what is going on in your church. By keeping your calendar up-to-date, you give people the ability to see what is going on and join in with your worship, Bible studies, and events. Not keeping them updated makes it appear as if you don't have the time to share with those stopping in at your website. Work to keep it up-to-date.

Your website is an incredible resource . . . for incredible resources! People hop online, find your church, and are looking to know more. If those people are Millennials, they are going to be able to scour all the nooks and crannies of your website. Why not take a moment and introduce them to some of the great resources you have at your disposal?

The first great resource your website has is the preaching and teaching that happens on a weekly basis. If you have the capability, you should record your sermons. Why? Because then you can let people hear the teaching from your church before they attend. They get to engage with your weekly teachings from the comfort and safety of their own home. This may seem like a trivial thing, but it is amazing how many times people tell us that they checked out our sermons before coming to our church.

A blog is another great way to share your church's resources. The price of printing can be cost-prohibitive for many churches. But with your website, you can easily set up a blog. Release the information that way. Millennials engage on their phones and computers. A blog is a quick and simple way to share information, teaching, or a devotion for the seasons of the Church Year.

When you start releasing resources, you make a promise to post on a regular schedule. We can't tell you how many well-meaning or incredible resources fall short because a church simply stops posting them regularly or posts so erratically that people lose interest. But if you can stick to your schedule, people will check in on that resource according to its schedule, whether it is weekly, monthly, or by season of the year.

Your website also gives you a chance to share your core values and beliefs as a church. Want people to know what you believe about the Sacraments before they walk in? Post them on your website. Want to help them understand your connection to the local community? Make sure your calendar is up-to-date with your service events. Your website is the new church sign, but it communicates so much more than the quick one-liners a sign can make.

A website should be built to tell your story as a church. The last several ideas all communicated guidelines on things your church should be doing with your website, but the greatest opportunity is to share the story of your church. Your web presence can be the first place that people hear the story of Jesus and what He is doing in the life of your church. There are a couple of great ways to do this that connect with Millennials in some great ways as well.

Make sure your staff and leadership volunteers are listed on your website along with their stories. Here is the formula we use at our church: Growing Up + Jesus in Your Life + Your Journey Here.

What does that look like? Here is my story from our church website:

I grew up as the middle of three kids, born on the western slopes of the Rocky Mountains in Craig, CO. When I was still very young, my family moved to a suburb just north of Houston, which I consider my childhood home. I have a deep fondness for Houston sports teams and the woods in which I ran around in our neighborhood as a kid.

Jesus claimed me in Baptism as a baby, and my life has been a constant growing process since then. I would classify myself as a recovering Pharisee, the product of my own need to prove that I am good enough. Because of this, Romans 5:6–8 has been a major theme in my life. I am constantly learning that there is nothing I can do to earn the love of God, but that in fact He has given it to me freely through Jesus. My daily walk in faith continually leads me back to learning what it means for Jesus to become greater and for me to become less, and to be able to see how that leads to my joy.

My journey would take me from Houston to Austin to attend Concordia University Texas. There, I spent my college years working with various ministries connected to the university. After graduation, I spent time as a high school youth minister at my home church before marrying my wife, Chelsey, in 2010. Moving from the heart of Texas to the Midwest, I attended Concordia Seminary in St. Louis and graduated in 2014.

Your story is important to people. It is important for others to see that your church is made up of personal stories that create the Body of Christ in your local community. For example, my sample biography not only gives facts about my life, but it also expresses some of my personality. It shows the importance of the Gospel in my life, while also admitting that I am not perfect and God is still at work in me. It is authentic. We'll talk more about that in a moment.

Allowing staff, leaders, elders, and others to tell their stories begins to tell the story of your church, but there are some other key ways to keep the narrative going.

» Beliefs—Take some time and figure out a solid but brief statement of beliefs for your church. Perhaps you could do this within your leadership structure. The key is an ironclad belief statement in 700 words or less (we just made up that word count to let you know to try and keep it brief). There is nothing worse than getting onto a church's website to find a belief statement that is so long it would take a doctorate to understand. You are not giving the whole counsel of God here. We'd encourage you to hit the main points: the Gospel, the Word, the Sacraments, and throw in a creed. If you want to add more information, try to refrain from doing so on this page. Remember, Twitter was invented by and for Millennials so they could communicate in 140 *characters* or less. It's not that we can't consume more information than that; we are just used to getting the gist of information quickly online. Setting up a "Want to Learn More?" link with online resources (maybe some you have created) allows us to dig deeper of our own volition instead of trying to read between the lines. This might also be the place to link to a deeper understanding of the Sacraments with an ability to contact someone for more information.

» Visiting—Put this on the front page! Give people all the pertinent information about what a visit to your church would look like. This is especially important if you meet somewhere besides your own building, or if there is a strange way to enter from the parking lot, or if there is some confusion as to where/when worship begins. Make sure to keep this updated for special seasons such as Advent, Christmas, Lent, Holy Week, and Easter. This immediately communicates that you like to welcome new people to your church. As a church-planting couple, Chelsey and I were given the opportunity during the first month and a half of our call to visit other church plants in the area to learn from what they were doing. Some we called beforehand, and some we showed up at unannounced, slipping in and out.

The websites that had instructions or suggestions on "How to Plan a Visit" were the best. It is hard to walk up to a church where you don't know anyone and try to find your place among the crowd.

» Another means of telling the story of your church? Your own people. Do not use stock photos of random people to represent your church. You may use stock photos for a graphic or for an event, but when you are publishing your website, avoid using stock "people" photos for pages on the site. Remember, Millennials can smell marketing a mile away. But what a great opportunity to share the life of your church! If you have the money, hire a photographer to come out for a Sunday to get some shots of people in worship, in Sunday School, or talking over coffee. If you don't have the money, see if there are any aspiring photographers in your congregation. Ask if they wouldn't mind shooting for you on a Sunday. These are not posed pictures; they are snapshots of the life of your church. When you do a service event, ask people to grab some pictures on their phone and send them to you. Use real people. The people of your church tell your story.[24]

Building a website is becoming less complicated and more affordable by the day. If your website is outdated, there are some incredible options for receiving help in constructing a new one. You might find a group that may be more hands-on and charge you a larger fee. If you are in need of saving some money and having a learning curve, you can build your own website fairly simply. Millennials know you are not a multibillion-dollar corporation; they are not expecting you to pull off the newest, coolest website. Instead, they are expecting you to be you. Just try to make it clean and welcoming, a site that tells your story and the story of Jesus.

---

24 A quick disclaimer: some people do not want their photo, or especially pictures of their kids, shared on the Internet. Do the best you can to ask permission, or share pictures with the folks in them a week ahead of time, so people can opt out if they so choose.

On a technical side, there are two options when it comes to updating your website. You can build it and maintain it yourself, or you can pay someone to do those things for you. Doing it yourself will cost you time but save you money. Paying someone else will cost you money but save you time.

If you need a website update, here are a couple of resources for you:

- **www.squarespace.com**—A web service with a simple set-up and intuitive user interface. Square Space is at the lower cost of the spectrum and is on the easier side of using. It might take some research to see how to use Square Space to build a church website, but Google is your friend!

- **Wordpress**—Wordpress started as a simple blogging site but has become so much more. This would move into the inter-mediate to intermediate-expert level of website building. You won't have to code, but you will have to learn a more intensive user interface and be able to navigate a larger learning curve of how to work in themes, buy a domain, and update your site. Again, Google is your friend.

- **Theme Forest**—This website sells website themes for Word-press. You can log in and search for church website themes. It will be important to realize that installing a theme does not mean you immediately get the look you are going for, but with practice, tutorials, and time you will have a great-looking website.

Want to check out some great church websites for inspiration? Head on over to **medium.com/thesidebar** for a list.

Social Media

Here it is—the pinnacle of Millennial online connection. Social me-dia can be your greatest online ally or your worst Internet nightmare. Because (and there is no way around this) Millennials are judging you on social media. The amount of social media consumed by Millennials daily could fill Uncle Scrooge's gold silo[25] several times over. If you don't get that reference, go find a few Millennials and ask them about it. Just know it is an exorbitant amount. In this day and age, to connect online with this generation, social media is a must. However, make sure you seek to do it well.

Let's do a quick overview of the main social media platforms.

- **Facebook**—Probably the king, for now, of social media. It was the one that put social media on the map, and it is not going away anytime soon. Facebook is a great place to touch base with your entire church. You can easily build a page for your church (not a personal profile, a page), publicize locally, and add events for your church. Facebook is great for sharing events, publishing videos, or even using their live feature (just make sure you have a plan).

- **Twitter**—No one imagined that so much could be communicated within 140 characters. Twitter proved everyone wrong. Great for quick thoughts or quotes, asking questions, and seeking responses.

- **Instagram**—Owned by Facebook, Instagram is a picture-sharing app that continues to grow. It's a wonderful way to share stories. Using their story function is great! I have started handing my phone off to one of our middle schoolers and asking her to build a story during worship on Sundays; it really works well!

All of these social media platforms have positive aspects. All of these social media platforms have negative drawbacks.

We are not going to tell you how or which one you should use. This might be a good time to talk to some Millennials in your church or

---

25   This is Uncle Scrooge from *DuckTales*, as opposed to Ebenezer Scrooge from Dickens's classic. The most memorable part of the opening song of *DuckTales* is Uncle Scrooge diving in for a swim in his silo filled with gold.

community about social media. What we will tell you is that it is important for you to be connected somehow and to use social media for your benefit.

Choose 2 Principle

Here we want to introduce you to what we will call the "Choose 2 Principle." This is not scientific, studied, or peer-reviewed. We have observed it in the experience of our church and other churches we know. It is tempting to try to jump on every social media platform. It gets even harder when the regular old media starts declaring a new platform the "Facebook Killer." Instead of jumping at everything new or trying to get your bearings on every form of social media, choose two. Find rhythm with two of them. Again, when you post on social media as an organization you are making a promise to be consistent. Some churches have the ability to hire someone for communications, thus someone to run their social media accounts. They may be able to handle more than two platforms, but in most places focusing on one or two forms of social media will be the most beneficial.

Remember you aren't trying to be the best content creators around. You are trying to be the best version of your church you can be on social media, and to connect with a generation who lives in the social media world.

Authentic

This brings us to the greatest piece of practical advice we can give you when it comes to connecting with Millennials as a church: be authentic.

You might think *authenticity* has become a buzzword, so you simply ignore it. You are probably right about it being a buzzword, but that doesn't mean you should ignore it. The thing mentioned most often when we talked to Millennials about this book, asking them what they looked for in a church, was authenticity. They want to be part of churches that aren't trying to be something they are not. In this chapter, we have given you some ideas for cleaning up your image and becoming more attractive and welcoming to the Millennial generation. What we are not saying is that you should try to be something you are not.

In all of your online interactions, from your website to social media, be authentic. Let your church be your church. Stop trying to compare your church to the next one down the road or to one down the street.

MILLENNIALS, I HAVE NOW RUN OUT OF CLEVER THINGS TO SAY, BUT COME OVER HERE.

Help with this. If we are so big on authenticity, let's be authentic. But let's remember that authenticity includes the taming of our tongues, that every idea we have is not good nor beneficial. It is easy to complain about how our churches just don't get it, how the website is from 1992, and we are not sure if the person running the Facebook page knows how to record in landscape on their phone. But let's be authentic. Let's explain why these things are important and why we care about them. And if we truly care about authenticity, let's not make it a buzzword that doesn't apply to us. Let's be authentic.

A Quick Soapbox

I am going to hop up on my soapbox one more time. As a church planter, there is one thing a church plant can do that will send me into orbit faster than a Saturn V rocket, and that is when they use some kind of tagline, mantra, or marketing statement that tears down another church. Instead of saying, "This is who Jesus is; this is who we are; here is why you should join us!" They say, "Look, we are not *THAT* church!" This is the most inauthentic way to tell people who you are. Instead of leading with comparison, lead with Jesus, and then with you.

God has worked in the local, physical community you are in to plant an outpost of His kingdom there. It is your church. Be your church. Stop trying to be someone else's church. We are not saying that you stop trying to grow and develop as a church. That would deny the work of the Holy Spirit in sanctification. Instead, we are saying that Millennials can tell when you are faking it. They know when you are putting on a show. They can smell it from a mile away.

The Importance of Telling the Story

A Millennial's keen sense of sniffing out anything fake is why we have suggested that you focus on story as an organization. Instead of telling Millennials the story you think they want to hear, tell them the story of Jesus and of who you are. Let every decision you make as an organization move that story into the world, warts and all.

All this talk of cleaning up your image is not to change your story; instead, it is to learn to tell it better. It is to give you insight. What would have happened had Luther not embraced the printing press? His and the early reformers' use of new technology got their message out. It didn't change their story; it just made it more accessible to those around them.

But why should you care? Why bother with these silly things? In fact, why even care about this book? It's simple: your story is important. The story of your church is important. Connecting Millennials to those stories is important.

Why?

Because everything we do, from mentoring to updating websites, from building relationships to being on social media, we do to connect people with the story of Jesus. Jesus tells us over and again that it is His joy to seek and to save that which is lost, to bring those who are far off near, to see the dead come alive. If *that* is Jesus' joy—and no servant is greater than their master—then it is our joy to see these things as well.

All this talk of cleaning up your image is not to change your story; instead, it is to learn to tell it better.

Millennials are falling away from the Church. But do not fear, little flock. It is the joy of the Father to give us the Kingdom.

And the stories of that Kingdom and its King in our lives are worth sharing.

DISCUSSION QUESTIONS

1. Take a hard look at your church's website, publications, and social media. Is there anything that you can help to clean and make more attractive?

2. Talk with Millennials and ask them what they would look for in social media from a church.

3. Take a minute and write your bio using the formula mentioned in this chapter:

Growing Up

Jesus in Your Life

Your Journey Here

DO IT

Tell your story. Tell it through relationships, mentoring, community, and an online presence. Tell your story because your story always points back to the Savior.

GLOSSARY

Adulting—The verb for "being an adult." Connected with new experiences or the added responsibilities of growing up. For example, "Today I mowed the lawn, replaced my car battery, and paid my taxes. A full day of *adulting*."

Amazon Prime Now—Amazon's delivery service that, in certain cities, will have your order to you within several hours as opposed to several days.

The Babylon Bee—The Christian version of the parody news website The Onion.

Buzzfeed—Describes itself as a "social news and entertainment company." Buzzfeed has everything from the day's news to quizzes, such as "Which Pop Tart flavor are you based on your Zodiac sign?"

Emojis—Small digital images used to express emotions or ideas.

GIF—Graphics Interchange Format. Basically a quick snippet of a video made into recurring images. Great for texting.

Grubhub—Don't want to go out and pick up food from your favorite restaurant for you? Grubhub will deliver, often even if the restaurant doesn't do delivery.

Hulu—A media streaming website.

Lit—Exciting, full of energy; an exclamation of something with those qualities. You can get lit or describe something as being lit.

The Onion—A parody news website.

Redditor—A registered user of the website Reddit, a giant website used for the sharing of content and discussion.

Roasting—Roasting is not a new thing. Think of Dean Martin's old TV roasts. Now imagine that happening constantly on social media.

theSkimm—A media company founded in 2012 that delivers the news to subscribers.

Snowflake—A derogatory term for someone who is perceived to have their feelings hurt too easily.

#sorrynotsorry—A phrase that is a sarcastic un-apology, as in, "I know there are a lot of fans of *Friends* out there, but *Parks and Rec* is better #sorrynotsorry."

Twitter—A micro blogging website. Every "tweet" can be only 140 characters long.

Uber—The new age of taxis. Uber is an app-based ride-sharing service where people use their own cars to drive other people around.

Yelp—A website used to rate local businesses. Ratings come from Yelpers, the users, as opposed to professional reviewers. This is an example of crowd-sourcing reviews.

About the Authors

Ted and Chelsey Doering both grew up in Texas. Ted was born in Colorado but spent most of his early life growing up in a suburb of Houston. Meanwhile, Chelsey grew up just north of Austin in the beautiful Texas Hill Country. Chelsey was a state spelling champion, drum major, and president of the student council in high school. Ted played a little lacrosse, a little trumpet, and enjoyed causing a little trouble with his friends. It's lucky they met in college. They both attended Concordia University Texas. We could tell you a long story about how they met, but it involves some pizza and two *very* different ideas of what actually happened. Luckily for Ted, Chelsey fell for him, and they got married in the summer of 2010. After that, Chelsey would be the reason they were able to eat, working everything from customer service to being a barista, while Ted attended Concordia Seminary in St. Louis, Missouri. After Ted graduated in 2014, their first call was back to Texas to plant a church. That has been one of the most exciting and scary things either of them has ever done. In their spare time, Ted and Chelsey enjoy hiking, cooking (Chelsey), BBQing (Ted), working on house projects, and laughing at the antics of their dog, Gus.

You can follow them on twitter here: @theo_d and @chelsjoy.

ENDNOTES

i   Goldman Sachs, "Millennials: Coming of Age," Goldman Sachs, www.
goldmansachs.com/our-thinking/pages/millennials (accessed June 19,
2017).

ii   Michael Lipka, "Millennials Increasingly Are Driving Growth of 'Nones,'" Pew
Research (May 12, 2015), www.pewresearch.org/fact-tank/2015/05/12/mil-
lennials-increasingly-are-driving-growth-of-nones (accessed June 19, 2017).

iii "Persona," Dictionary.com, www.dictionary.com/browse/persona?s=t (accessed June 19, 2017).

iv   MarketingCharts, "Demographic Stats about US Millennials," Marketing-
Charts (February 24, 2014), www.marketingcharts.com/traditional/demo-
graphic-stats-about-us-millennials-40016 (accessed June 19, 2017).

v   "New American Community Survey Statistics," United States Census
Bureau (September 15, 2016), www.census.gov/newsroom/press-releas-
es/2016/cb16-159.html (accessed June 19, 2017).

vi   Goldman Sachs, "Millennials: Coming of Age."

vii Matt Chandler, "Following God May End Badly," YouTube, www.youtube.
com/watch?v=RhS2-K1EUBI (accessed June 19, 2017).

viii Ashley Abramson, "Millennials Are the Most Stressed-Out Generation.
And That's a Spiritual Problem," *Relevant Magazine* (June 10, 2016), www.
relevantmagazine.com/life/millennials-are-most-stressed-out-genera-
tion-and-s-spiritual-problem (accessed June 19, 2017).

ix   Associated Press, "Millennials Earn 20% Less than Boomers Did at Same
Stage of Life," *USA Today* (January 13, 2017), www.usatoday.com/story/
money/2017/01/13/millennials-falling-behind-boomer-parents/96530338/
(accessed June 19, 2017).

x   Sophia Tulp, "Is 'Working Your Way Through College' a Modern-Day Myth?"
USA Today College (August 1, 2016), college.usatoday.com/2016/08/01/is-
working-your-way-through-college-a-modern-day-myth (accessed June 19,
2017).

xi   college.usatoday.com/2016/08/01/is-working-your-way-through-college-a-
modern-day-myth/.

xii "Top 10 Collins Words of the Year 2016," Collins Dictionary, www.collins-dictionary.com/word-lovers-blog/new/top-10-collins-words-of-the-year-2016,323,HCB.html (accessed June 19, 2017).

xiii "Generation Snowflake," Wikipedia (last edited June 14, 2017), en.wikipedia.org/wiki/Generation_Snowflake (accessed June 19, 2017).

xiv Eleanor Halls, "Millennials. Stop Being Offended By, Like, Everything," *GQ* (August 12, 2016), www.gq-magazine.co.uk/article/millennials-created-generation-snowflake (accessed June 19, 2017).

xv Jeffrey Gottfried and Elisa Shearer, "News Use Across Social Media Platforms 2016," Pew Research Center (May 26, 2016), www.journalism.org/2016/05/26/news-use-across-social-media-platforms-2016/ (accessed June 19, 2017).

xvi Benjamin Mathes, "How to Listen When You Disagree: A Lesson from the Republican National Convention," Urban Confessional (July 27, 2016), urbanconfessional.org/blog/howtodisagree (accessed June 19, 2017).

xvii "Abadak Monster Chair," Abadak, www.abadak.com/abadak-monster-chair.html (accessed June 19, 2017).

xviii Melissa Etehad and Rob Nikolewski, "Millennials and Car Ownership? It's Complicated," *Los Angeles Times* (December 23, 2016), www.latimes.com/business/autos/la-fi-hy-millennials-cars-20161223-story.html (accessed June 19, 2017); Yuki Noguchi, "Fewer Young People Buying Houses, But Why?" *All Things Considered* (July 26, 2016), www.npr.org/2016/07/26/487470787/fewer-young-people-buying-houses-but-why (accessed June 19, 2017).

xix Carlos Beltrán, "Why I'm Coming Back to Houston," *The Players' Tribune* (January 10, 2017), www.theplayerstribune.com/carlos-beltran-astros/ (accessed June 19, 2017).

xx Robert Kolb, Timothy J. Wengert, and Charles P. Arand, *The Book of Concord: The Confessions of the Evangelical Lutheran Church* (Minneapolis, MN: Fortress Press, 2000), 38–40.

xxi Kolb, Wengert, and Arand, *The Book of Concord*, 40.